T0383427

Contemporary
Café Design●

A COFFEE A DAY

Contemporary
Café Design●

Chris van Uffelen

# A COFFEE A DAY

BRAUN

# CAFÉS+ARCHITECTS

CONTENTS

# ESSAYS

# APPENDIX

CONTENTS

# PREFACE

# CAFFEINE AND CONVERSATION

Keep calm and drink coffee! This roasted beverage accompanies the daily lives of a large proportion of adults worldwide. About 2.25 billion cups are being consumed daily, cherished for the aroma and caffeine content. Whether you just like it as a kick starter in the morning or can't get enough of it throughout the day; whether you take your time to drink it or grab a cup on the way – there are endless possibilities regarding the production, trade, roasting, preparing, and serving of this black gold. Over time, coffee has found its way from the Middle East of the 16th century into virtually every household, having become widely available and affordable as well. But the homemade cup doesn't compare to the experience of visiting a coffee house. Embedded in the acoustic backdrop of conversations, music, and clattering from the bar, customers can soak in the design of the interior while savoring the smell and taste of their expertly prepared coffee. Of course, this simple observation can't adequately grasp all facets that come with this special location and its rich history. For centuries now, coffee houses have been evolving and thereby serving all sorts of purposes besides preparing and drinking coffee. They can be sanctuaries for relaxation keeping out the chores of everyday routine or a space where business is done, and political opinions are formed. Moreover, they can incorporate various sorts of entertainment like live music, board games, or newspapers. With elaborated designs, coffee houses can transport customers to another period or resemble places like museums, gardens, or lakes. Over the years, they have evolved into multi-purpose locations that can be adapted to the needs of the event at hand, or hybrid spaces that offer not only coffee but other products and services. But most importantly coffee houses have always been places of social gathering and exchange. All of this was suddenly disrupted by the outbreak of the COVID-19-pandemic in 2020, when people were instructed to stay at home due to safety measures. Since then, public locations like coffee houses stopped being something taken for granted. This book brings coffee house culture back to memory, portraits designs from all over the world, and gives hope for a future in which enjoying a cup of coffee in a coffee house is as convenient and safe as it was before.

PREFACE

A

| | |
|---|---|
| Architect | YOD GROUP |
| Graphic Designer | PRAVDA DESIGN |
| Location | KYIV— UKRAINE |
| Year of Completion | 2021 Gross floor area/seats 30,6M2/10 |

DOT Coffee Station #1 is a city café that specializes in high-quality coffee drinks to go. It is located in central Kyiv, on the street that borders Bessarabska Square, a vibrant point in one of the city's most active neighborhoods.

The interior design focuses on mosaic pixel art on the walls, that incorporates the dot as a pixel theme. It evokes a weird, sincere, and universal emotion manifesting modern city life. The location's dynamic rhythm is also reflected by narrow LED-screens displaying scrolling text. The stairs and part of the wall surface are covered with white mosaic tiles. Other walls show the bare brick that highlights the value of the building, erected in 1900.

The architects decided to show the 4.75-meter-high ceiling instead of building a mezzanine with additional seating spaces. Glass sliding doors create a transparent façade and let the room fill up with light, emphasizing the venue's hospitality. The café has two little tables and a niche with a bench where a few guests can sit. Another seating place is the massive bench along with the building façade next to the café. The timber of both benches and the counter reuse old beams that used to be elements of a barn a long time ago. It is a time-proven material that tells its own story and works as a contrast with the perfect and cold elements made of stainless steel ●

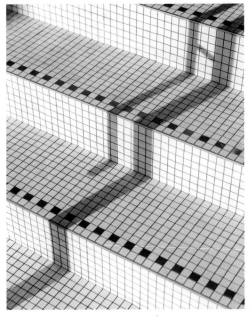

B

DOT COFFEE STATION #1

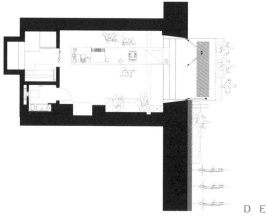

D E

F G

DOT COFFEE STATION #1

A

Architect **BWM ARCHITEKTEN**

Location **VIENNA — AUSTRIA**

Year of Completion **2018** Gross floor area/seats **70M2/40**

A  general view of Salon Sacher
B  oval bar, accented by curved globe lights
C  detailed view of wall, bench, and black-and-white-patterned floor
D  floor plan
E  tent-like ceiling vault with stucco

Following the redesign of the Sacher Eck at the end of 2017, BWM Architekten have also redesigned the former Sacher Stube, now known as the Salon Sacher. The black and coral color scheme and the 1920s and 1950s elements congenially complement one another. Arched globe lights highlight the bar's role as a centerpiece, while tinted mirrors, black lines, and metallic effects perfectly round off the overall look. The preserved stucco ceiling is an absolute eyecatcher: Previously hidden behind the dropped ceiling, this historic jewel was discovered during the construction work. A large section of it is now displayed in all its splendor. The tent-like structure of the room dissolves the usual spatial boundaries, creating an impression of surprising vastness. The central theme is also consistently reflected in the furnishings. The original Thonet chairs have been restored and reupholstered; the tables have partly been left in their original state, keeping their brass bases while being furnished with new stone tabletops.

The geometric lines and black and white pattern of the floor are inspired by a sketch by the famous architect Josef Hoffmann, who was one of the co-founders of the Wiener Werkstätte as well. Black is also the color of the vertical trim-edges on the walls, ceiling, and the wainscot panelling. Together, all these elements create a contrast to the lightness of the coral-colored upholstery.

The dominant element of the interior design is the new, oval bar with a surface consisting of a stone slab set in brass and sides clad with bronze-colored, facetted mirror strips – all emphasized by arched globe lights, designed by the Viennese designer Megumi Ito. The crowning glory is the historical stucco ceiling tantalizingly peeking out of the oval opening while a neon border draws all eyes to it ●

B

C

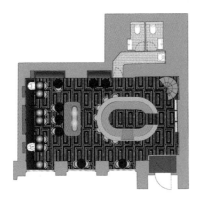

SALON SACHER

Architect MODISTE STUDIO

Location BERLIN — GERMANY

Year of Completion 2020 Gross floor area/seats 43M2/20

A

A exterior view
B counter area with shelving
  system
C floor plan
D green marble floor
E detail of retail display and
  storage
F interior with timber
  furniture

The new outpost of Bonanza Coffee Roasters in Berlin's Mitte-quarter is a contemporary tribute to the coffee bars of Milan with a sense of tradition. True to Modiste Studio's design dogma the architects only used three main materials – stone, steel, and timber. The central element is a freeform shape in hand-polished stainless steel, made by expert craftspeople in the north of the Netherlands. 55 square meters of the finest green marble were used for the floor and all work surfaces. A bespoke shelving system in the shop and behind the counter is used as retail displays and as much needed storage in this small café in one of the nicest streets of Berlin-Mitte. Modiste designed and built all be-spoke furniture and everything for Bonanza, except for five stools by Hans Wegner ●

.B

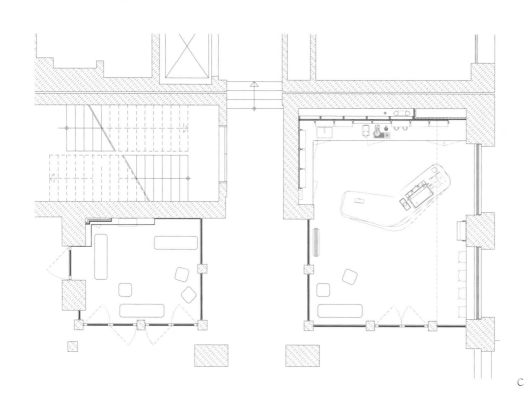

C

D E      F

... GENDARMENMARKT

A

Architect  TEMP.

Location  BEIJING — CHINA

Year of Completion  2020  Gross floor area/seats  180M2/30

In Beijing the architecture studio temp. combined Amoon Optical, which is known as one of the most professional optical glasses store in the city, with a café. The store design plays with repeating elements of basic geometric circles and curves to shape the space. Arches, walls, and a set of circular screens made by strings connect the entire space into one whole, yet divide zones into smaller private areas. The screens can be re-arranged for different situations as they are put together by rotating hinges. The C-shaped bar and the bamboo screens also naturally divide the glasses area and the main café space.

During busy hours the consulting tables for prescribing optical glasses can also function as café seating. The architecture studio also custom-designed chairs from bamboo, using mortise and tenon joints as well as traditional craft widely available from Anji in the South of China. Mirrors are used to reflect spaces and for customers to try on the glasses. They are at the same time strategically placed to create an illusion of duplicating the glasses display made by brass and wood. With its design the store attempts to translate the idea of glasses as a highly calibrated result between form and function ●

AMOON OPTICAL CAFÉ

B

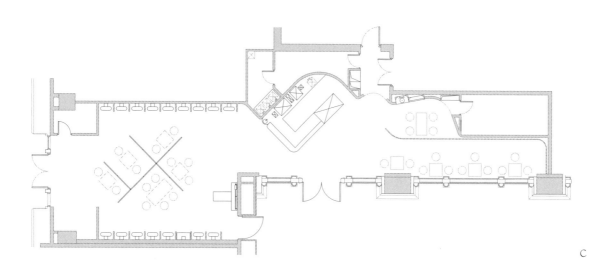

C

D    E

AMOON OPTICAL CAFÉ

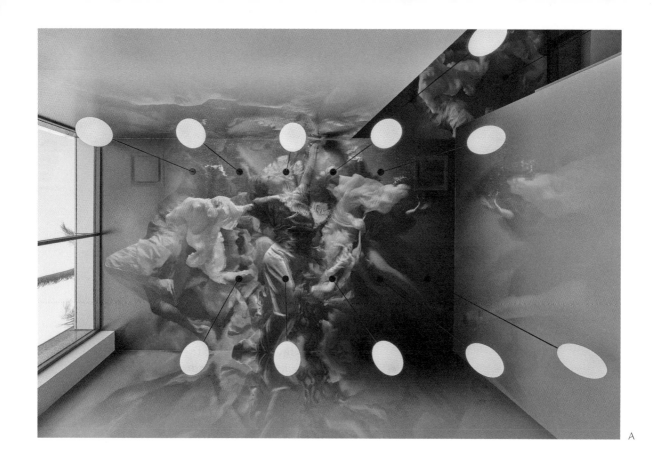

A

Architect WICK ARCHITECTURE &
DESIGN, LAND DESIGN STUDIO
Location NEWPORT BEACH, CA — USA
Year of Completion 2020 Gross floor area/seats 62,5M2/13

STEREOSCOPE COFFEE

Stereoscope is a branded coffee shop in Newport Beach that is turning heads with its cathedral-like opulence. The Newport Beach location is the second store opening for Stereoscope Coffee in Orange County, and raises the bar on the modern coffee shop experience for the roaster's sophisticated coffee clientele.

The coffee shop is situated on the ground level of a large two-building office complex sharing a common courtyard. The L-shaped space connects to entrances at both ends of the L, including one adjacent to the building's lobby, and another connecting to the exterior courtyard. The layout, together with Stereoscope Coffee's taste for modern minimalism, created a unique challenge for Wick Architecture & Design, in partnership with Land Design Studio.

Having traveled the world extensively, David Wick and Andrew Lindley harkened back to a recent trip to Italy, where they had the opportunity to view Correggio's "Assumption of the Virgin", a 16th-century fresco adorning the dome of the Cathedral of Parma. The duo envisioned the possibility of a modern interpretation and adaptation of that historic Renaissance approach, with a multi-dimensional aspect added to it. This would capture the essence of stereoscopy, a precursor to modern 3D technology. Christy Lee Rogers, an artist who is renowned for her unique underwater Renaissance and Baroque style photography, approached with the idea of licensing a piece of her work, "The Reunion of Cathryn Carrie and Jean", and then transferring it to 3D. The art was printed on vinyl rolls. Once completed, they were applied to the ceiling like wallpaper in a remarkable installation process that took less than a day to complete.

In contrast to the boldness of the cathedral-like ceiling, Stereoscope's interior is warm and modern. White oak bench seating wraps around the L-shaped space. Visible from both entrances, blue orca marble infuses movement and texture into the cut stone coffee bar's minimalist composition ●

B

C

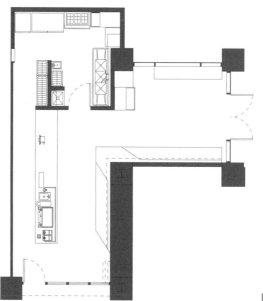

D E                                    F

STEREOSCOPE COFFEE

Architect **PARTY / SPACE / DESIGN SC**

Location **BANKOK — THAILAND**

Year of Completion **2021** Gross floor area/seats **450M2/200**

A

Rolling Roasters is not only a café, but also a coffee roastery for various suppliers. This had a decisive influence on the design, because customers can see and smell the process of roasting, move between the storing bags of coffee, which are part of the design. The theme of the design is "aging": the rooms should look old, rustic and classic, although the place itself was not. The former bread factory, was abandoned shortly after construction was completed so it had to be artificially aged. The iron was rusted by acid, the wood got its texture by flaming. Even all the marks that can be seen on the wooden parts were made by spraying or scraping by hand. Guests can sit in the garden or on an upper floor designed as a vantage point from which to view the café and roasting from above ●

ROLLING ROASTERS

B

HERE'S THE FUTURE EXPERIMENTED

HE FUTURE ...CES THE PRESENT JUST AS MUCH

C

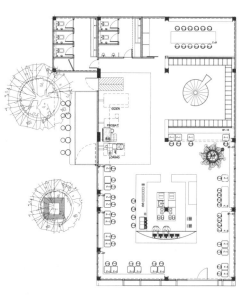

D E      F

ROLLING ROASTERS

A

Architect **OBRA VERDE**

Location **CARACAS — VENEZUELA**

Year of Completion **2019** Gross floor area/seats **33M2/14**

Quiero1Café is a specialty coffee shop located in Los Palos Grandes, an area in Caracas, which boomed with new commercial businesses and urban life. After several years of existing as a pop-up bar, the café hired Obra Verde to create the brand's first brick and mortar store.

The architects implemented design elements, construction processes and techniques, which are representative of the artisanal processes of coffee production. An L-shaped espresso and brew bar fills up the space and facilitates interaction between customers and baristas. The coffee roaster is placed in the back and serves as the visual focus of the room. The linear spotlight system, as well as the tables with benches and bar stools, were custom-designed and arranged in a harmonious fashion to create different customer experiences within the small space. The finishing elements and construction materials were all sourced from local producers. The bar's countertop was built on site with a three-piece gray terrazzo, while new walls were built with red clay blocks filled with cement. Natural pine plywood and black metal profiles were the materials selected for the furniture. A handcrafted, ceramic mural, extending from the main wall to the bathroom, serves as another highlight element. The project was complemented with natural indoor plants and the brand's coffee related decorative objects, while coffee objects such as filter holders were used in design elements like doorknobs. The result is a cozy and simple space filled with details, designed to encourage the enjoyment of coffee culture and contemporary Venezuelan design ●

QUIERO1CAFÉ

B

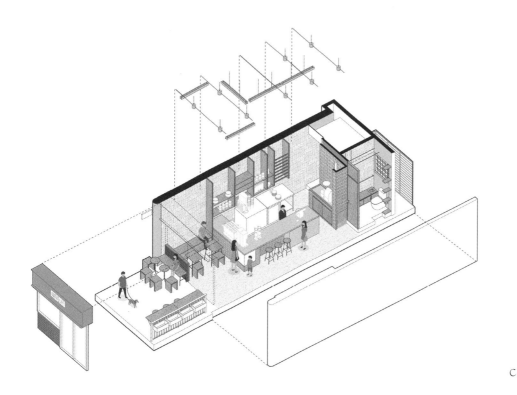

C

D E                                                      F

QUIERO1CAFÉ

| | |
|---|---|
| Architect | CUT ARCHITECTS |
| Location | PARIS — FRANCE |
| Year of Completion | 2020 |
| Gross floor area/seats | 81M2/44 |

A

B

The gallery café Coutume is a Parisian roaster with the commitment to offer specialty coffees, accompanied with the terroir of their production, to their roasting and extraction, while respecting their origin and seasonality. The Galeries Lafayette, an iconic Parisian venue, offered the roaster a majestic space overlooking the emblematic Art Deco dome. The challenge of this project was to reveal Coutume without distorting its environment. In order to integrate it coherently into the architectural heritage, typical Parisian features from zinc to moldings were adopted. Like a luminous thread, an illuminated tubular structure runs along the counter and highlights this revisited zinc. Cut architects also expressed the values of custom by deploying a vocabulary of forms and materials derived from the repertoire of the archetypal Parisian café ●

COUTUME ...

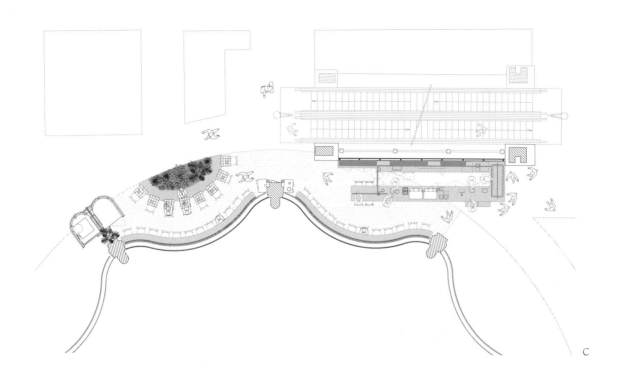

C

D          E

... GALERIES LAFAYETTE

A

Architect NONESPACE

Location SEONGSAN-EUP —
SOUTH KOREA

Year of Completion 2020  Gross floor area/seats 369M2/250

A  fabric objects in second
   floor café hall
B  façade made of volcanic
   stone
C  seating with sea view
D  mountain stairway
E  first and second floor plan

Seongsan-eup, located on the east side of Jeju volcanic island, borders the sea and its spectacular rock formations. Here the architects wanted to create a space where guests can interact with nature while also infusing traditional and regional sentiments. The exterior blocks, interior furniture, and walls, are volcanic stones that embody the heavy and crude indigenous esthetics of Jeju. The first floor consists of a café bar and a promenade, and the second floor consists of a café hall, a terrace, and an external stairway to the first floor.

Upon arrival on the first floor, a natural promenade can be seen spreading out. Due to the accumulation of space, the entryway on the left passes through the unique Road of Light which is reminiscent of a subtropical region. Different scenes unfold each time. It faces the west side which is opposite the sea. When walking to the north, a spacious garden containing silver grass, citrus, and rapeseed flowers can be seen through a window and it leads to an outside promenade.

When entering the second floor – after passing the mountain stairway and the central stairs, that seem to lead to the sky – fabric objects can be seen together with the sea and the walls. There are windows on the south and north sides to create a breeze, using an ultra-thin yarn material to let the wind through. The back side, adjacent to the window, was created with a slight step, considering the view of the sea by ensuring a level difference. In the back, the courtyard was designed so that customers can experience the light of Jeju as well as the bamboo forest. With most of the windows located on the east side, the space, which could have ended up cold, turned out to be clear and warm, based on the light and landscape embodied by the courtyard. The space brings in the scenery of Jeju, such as its stones, sea, wind, sky, light, and trees as ordinary objects, and aims to show the ecology and demise of extraordinary nature ●

CAFÉ OOO

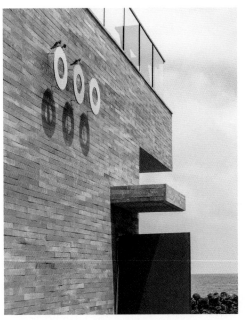

B

C

D

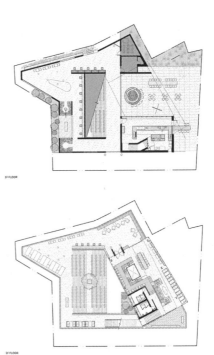

1F FLOOR

2F FLOOR

E

CAFÉ OOO

Architect **IPPOLITO FLEITZ GROUP —
IDENTITY ARCHITECTS**
Location **STUTTGART — GERMANY**
Year of Completion **2019** Gross floor area/seats **62M2/22**

A

B

A general view of the main
   space
B detailed view of the
   counter
C floor plan
D façade and sitting area
E sitting area with
   chic painting

Home to over 6,000 plant species and over
1,200 animals, the Wilhelma in Stuttgart is
one of the most visited zoological-botanical
gardens in Germany. Nestled between aviar-
ies and greenhouses, right next to the
Moorish Pavilion, is a small sanctuary for
snacking and relaxing: Caffè Belvedere. The
concept behind the café was primarily about
bridging the gap between sophistication and
simplicity, with the long tradition of the
Wilhelma reflected in the ambience as well
as the down-to-earth character of its guests.
Every detail of the complete transformation
of the 1960s, listed building has been lovingly considered and designed. Traditional
Italian elements infuse the room with joy of
life; the orange covered diner bench with ca-
sualness. Indoor swings complete the touch
of lightness ●

CAFFÈ BELVEDERE

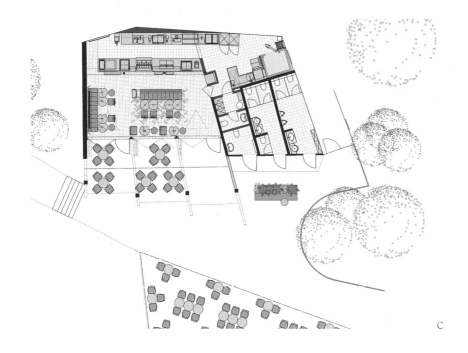

C

D          E

CAFFÈ BELVEDERE

# BLACK AS HELL

# COFFEE HOUSE
# HISTORY

Imagine wandering the city streets of metropolises like Vienna, Paris or Budapest, where traditional coffee houses with waiters in suits line up with ultra-modern coffee shops that rather appear like open-plan offices or research labs for coffee brewing. One might wonder about these apparent contrasts, but the history of coffee houses has always been a fascinating interplay of tradition and modernity, functionality and aesthetic, as well as conservatism and rebellion. It shows, that the definition of a „coffee house" can never be a fixed one, since each establishment must be seen as a representation of its time and the history of coffee houses as the story of changing, developing societies.

The first coffee houses were reputedly established in Constantinople, today's Istanbul, in 1554. In modest shacks or tents with simple seating arrangements, guests looked on while ground coffee was poured into copper pots filled with hot water, balanced on top of tiled stoves whose fires burned continually. In 1647 the first coffee tavern in Western Europe was allegedly established in Vienna. As other big cities in Germany, the UK or the Netherlands followed soon after, dark and cramped beer taverns or shops, modified a little for their new purpose, often served as premises for these early enterprises.

A couple of decades later, the first sumptuously decorated, light-filled coffee houses began to appear. The international standard was set with Café Procope, established in Paris in 1686, with its tables made from slabs of marble and walls entirely of mirrors generating an illusion of vastness. The desire among the social elite of the period both to observe and to be observed had never been met quite so flamboyantly as in Café Procope, which inspired numerous similarly boastful coffee houses in the central squares and streets of towns such as Venice. In 1720, Caffè Florian opened its doors to coffee drinkers for the first time and, before long, no self-respecting tourist to the city could leave without paying a visit. During this period, coffee houses were stocked with copies of the most important national and local newspapers, which guests could read free of charge – it's now impossible to imagine a coffee house culture without this custom.

Caffè Florian
in Venice, Italy

Leading the way were England and the Netherlands with their strong democratic traditions, as well as pre-revolutionary, newly enlightened France. The middle classes of the 18th century were hungry for education and information. However, they also wanted to be entertained in these gatherings. As a result, card and board games as well as billiard tables became regular features of coffee house life. Some establishments even offered performances by singers and orchestras, or incorporated the brand new invention of cinema at the beginning of the 20th century. The emphasis on the bourgeois family in the Biedermeier era led to the dissolution of "men only" coffee houses in about 1870, replaced by family cafés that welcomed women. The public coffee culture was revolutionized, when "women only" cafés began to appear, often coupled with confectioner's shops. The bourgeois coffee house was no longer primarily a place for debates on politics and current affairs, but rather the epitome of comfort and relaxation. The presence of numerous establishments in every town and city in Europe was now taken for granted. In 1900, more than 600 could be found in Vienna alone and more than 500 in Budapest.

Scarcely any other image of coffee house culture has become so engrained in the popular imagination as that of a gathering place for artists, particularly literary figures. By the end of the 19th century, Viennese coffee houses were widely acknowledged as the epitome of coffee house culture, an achievement in which the city's literary figures played no small part. In 2011, UNESCO awarded the Viennese coffee house culture the status of World Heritage Site. At the end of the 1930s, the Parisian Café de Flore, open since 1865 and frequented by André Breton and the surrealists, became the center of French intellectual life. Jean-Paul Sartre wrote the majority of his key philosophical work by using the scenes around him to illustrate his abstract ideas. Simone de Beauvoir and Boris Vian also wrote in Café de Flore, while Pablo Picasso and Marc Chagall could often be found there engrossed in heated debates on art or scribbling quick sketches on the café's serviettes.

Caffé Florian on Piazza San Marco

Café Griensteidl in Vienna, 1896

Laments about the end of the "real" coffee house are almost as old as the institution itself. Every change in taste and consumer demographic inspires woeful cries on the loss of the old and vocal assaults on the new as a sure sign of decay. There are of course still traditional coffee houses in which guests can enjoy a coffee and a newspaper in relaxed surroundings, just as in previous centuries. At the same time however, cafés and modern coffee shops since the 1980s – many of which belong to international chains – have been trying to respond to consumer demands in a hectic modern world. They are therefore functional and clearly designed with large counters, where guests are offered unlimited variations on the content, size, and aesthetics of their beverage. The interior is often more like a bar than a café, designed for people who will sit only briefly before moving on, drinking their coffee-to-go out of disposable paper cups with lids or taking it with them to drink on the move or in the office. Perhaps it is possible to say that while the ambience of coffee houses is in perpetual and unpredictable flux, the love of coffee among societies all over the world remains as strong as ever.

A

Architect ESTUDIO CHÁVARRO

Location CHIPAQUE — COLOMBIA

Year of Completion 2020  Gross floor area/seats 250M2/90

Café Mustapan has been around for over 60 years, located right in the main square of Chipaque, Colombia, a small town close to Bogota, the capital city of the country. The place prides itself in serving the best of traditional local bakery and attracts clients of all types. All kinds of people, from local farmers to tourists, take a seat everyday to have an arepa and a cup of coffee.

A unique identity, that aimed to respond to the countryside context, was delivered to the place by exposing the original adobe bricks, found in the patrimonial house. They were followed up by new concrete walls, handmade cement tiles and clay roofing tiles, among other materials that are distinctive to the area.

The design is the result of an extension of the place, in which some rooms of the neighboring property – actually the owner's home – were added, such as the original patio, typical of all colonial houses. In spite of not being right in the center of the café, the patio is the actual heart of it. This is where all materials inspired by the countryside meet, and where the gothical tower of Chipaque's church is visible: a direct visual link with the town.

Through the use of multiple typologies of chairs, tables and spaces to sit, visitors will have a different experience and perspective of the café, depending on the spot they choose to sit. Additionally, artificial lighting at night seeks to wrap clients in a very special and warm atmosphere, while still highlighting the architecture and materiality of the place ●

CAFÉ MUSTAPAN

B

CAFÉ MUSTAPAN

c

D

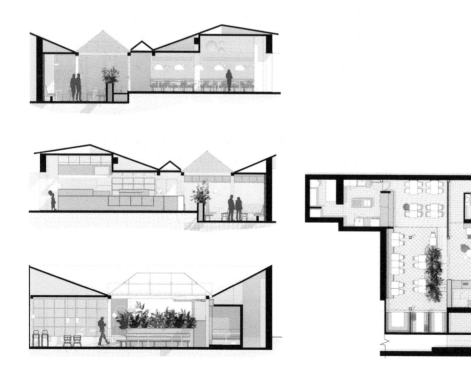

E          F

BEBIDAS FRÍAS
SI HAY AREPAS
PARA ACOMPAÑAR
Con café
TINTO
CAPUCHINO
MOCACINO
CHIPAQUE
Mustapán
DESDE 1958
Sin café

A

Architect **SGNHA**

Location **HO CHI MINH CITY — VIETNAM**

Year of Completion **2020**  Gross floor area/seats **220M2/80**

Okkio is a specialty coffee shop located in a small alley on Duy Tan Street. It occupies an old French colonial villa, an authentic half of a semidetached villa amongst a few that remain in the neighborhood. Duy Tan fondly recalls the memory of Saigon. Surviving the ups and downs of the city history, century-old parashorea trees stand tall along the pavements. Fortunately, the villa condition exceeds our expectation of time impact despite being quite aged.

Okkio means "eye" in Italian. Okkio considers himself as an observer, in the nowness, in between what is to happen and what has been gone. Its space consists of the front villa, a new two-story block at the back and a garden. All are connected by an enclosed walkway. The space is a dialogue between the old and the new. It contrasts by defining clear borders, or homogenizes by blurring joints. There is a conversation at every junction: at the dash between eras from Cochinchina – Bauhaus – present day, through the walkway coming from the old villa to the new block; at the demarcation between buildings and context; between exposed old-grey-solid brick wall and sand texture painted new wall; at the replacement of raw galvanized steel for broken window frames, door frames as well as the old balcony handrails; even the stainless-steel surfaces that blur the definition of 'new' materials.

The stainless-steel and cooper brew bar occupies most of the villa first floor. Concrete floor and skirting, applied to the whole villa, resemble the concrete steps of the original staircase. Coming upstairs to the second floor, one is immediately welcomed by natural states of materials: concrete floor and skirting, off-white sand texture painted and exposed old-grey-solid brick walls, raw galvanized steel, polished stainless steel, black leather and monochrome finish wood.

The garden is a buffer zone between the old villa and the new block. The walkway divides it into two parts: a patio and a courtyard. Glass louvers along the walkway subtly define the inside and the outside●

B

OKKIO DUY TAN CAFFE

D

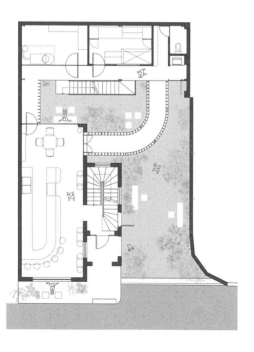

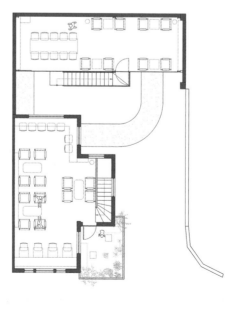

E  F          G

OKKIO DUY TAN CAFFE

| | |
|---|---|
| Architect | BUREAU EUGENIE ARLT |
| Location | VIENNA — AUSTRIA |
| Year of Completion | 2019 |
| Gross floor area/seats | 75M2/35 |

A

B

A wall graphic that was discovered during the
  renovation
B seating area with bar table
  in the back
C drawing
D seating area in front of the
  bar
E concrete bar with Slayer
  coffee machine

Balthasar Kaffee Bar is located in the second district of Vienna, Austria, and aims to create a relaxed, yet distinctive atmosphere. The tables, chairs, and benches were made by Hussl Tirol, with the tables having been custom designed for this project. The bar is made of dark-gray concrete slabs and serves as the central starting point of the café. It displays a Slayer coffee machine in the corporate identity colors. The walls behind the bar were painted in Galerie So's striking "Fiaker Schwarz" color, referring to the horse-drawn carriages so typical of Vienna. The graphic on this wall was uncovered and secured during the renovation, while the 5.5-meter-high vaulted ceiling was maintained. A bar table in the middle of the space is often used as a meeting point for guests to discuss the latest gossip of the neighborhood. With the objective of improving the situation in the countries of origin, the café trades directly with the coffee producers ●

BALTHASAR.
KAFFEE BAR

PERSPEKTIVES

GROSSFORMATIGE
PENDELLEUCHTE
VON UNTERZUG
ABGEHÄNGT

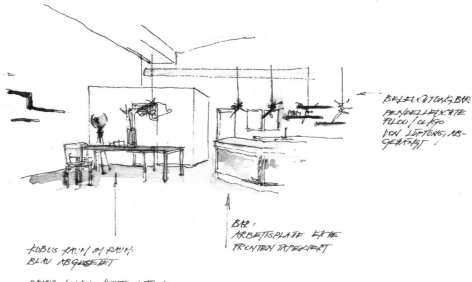

BELEUCHTUNG BAR
PENDELLEUCHTE
FLOU / OLIGO
VON LÜFTUNG AB-
GEHÄNGT

BAR:
ARBEITSPLATTE EICHE
FRONTEN TAPEZIERT

KUBUS KALT IM RAUM:
BLAU ABGESETZT

.DAVOR KOMMUNIKATIONSTISCH
—> PRODUKTPRÄSENTATION
—> SKIZTSCHUE
—> STÜHLE NACH BEDARF

C

D

E

SELBSTBEDIENUNG

| APFELSAFT WETTER | € |
| — II — GESPRITZT | 4,20 |
| CHARITEA | 3,50 |
| HOLLERSAFT | 3,10 |
| LEMONAID | 2,40 |
| FRITZ-KOLA | 3,10 |
| | 3,10 |
| SAUVIGNON BLANC | 1/8 LT. |
| STRABLEGG LEITNER | 3,90 |
| GRÜNER VELTLINER | |
| JÄGER | 3,90 |
| CRÉMANT ROSÉ | 0/1 LT. |
| HENRI KIEFFER | 5,80 |
| CHAMPAGNE | |
| POL ROGER | 8,90 |

BALTHASAR

KAFFEE BAR

BALTHASAR KAFFEE BAR

A

Architect **RGA STUDIO**

Location **MILAN — ITALY**

Year of Completion **2018** Gross floor area/seats **140M2/36**

A bar under Pietro Damini's "St. Bernard Converting the Duke of Aquitania"
B petrol blue walls, walnut tables and the sculpture "The Three Graces" by Bertel Thorvaldsen
C elevations
D floor plan
E detail of the bar – glass, brass and walnut
F the old entrance and the portrait of Fernanda Wittgens by Attilio Rossi

The Caffè Fernanda is part of a larger project to redesign the Pinacoteca di Brera and its collection. It is named after Fernanda Wittgens, the gallery's visionary director, who was responsible for its reopening in 1950, after the terrible bombings of 1943.

Located in the former main entrance, the café is conceived as a part and parcel of the museum tour. It echoes the new curation of the museum's 38 rooms by director James Bradburne, carried out over the past three years. Hence, the project finds a chromatic and material coherence with the gallery's new layout and forms a reinterpretation of the space's 1950s architecture. The intense petrol blue of the walls harmonizes with the warm hues of the gallery rooms and sets off the artworks exhibited in the café: Pietro Damini's "St. Bernard Converting the Duke of Aquitania", Bertel Thorvaldsen's "The Three Graces", the bust of Fernanda Wittgens by Marino Marini, and her portrait by Attilio Rossi. Adjustable LED projectors are the sole source of light, as befits the environment and the works. Recovered and restored, the splendid, peach-blossom marble floors and the Levanto-red frames – prominent features of Piero Portaluppi's previous design – remain untouched.

Below Damini's 17th-century painting is the café's large, round-edged bar. Its design evokes ribbed wooden furniture from the 1950s, albeit with inverted proportions: enlarged, semi-circular strips of canaletto walnut, topped by an uncharacteristically thin, antique-brass surface. The same brass, thinned even further, frames the large mirror, in which not only the bar's bottles, but fragments of Thorvaldsen's "Cupid and the Three Graces" are reflected. The tables, too, are made of brass and walnut. A certain material coherence guarantees the space its harmony. Lounging in the antique-pink and brass armchairs, one can admire Marini's bust, while the tables by the bar offer a privileged view of both Attilio Rossi's portrait and Francesco Hayez's famous "The Kiss", located in the final room of the gallery ●

B

CAFFÈ FERNANDA

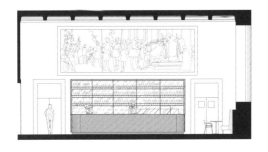

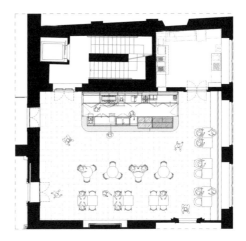

C D

E F

CAFFÈ FERNANDA

| | |
|---|---|
| Architect | ABOUT SPACE |
| Location | BERLIN — GERMANY |
| Year of Completion | 2018 |
| Gross floor area/seats | 5,76M2/50 |

A

A view from inside the cube
B courtyard with seating area
C isometric view
D detailed view of the glossy surface
E side view with neo-classical façades in the background

Kioski is reviving the modular space system K67, fifty years after it was designed by Slovenian architect Saša J. Mächtig. K67 was created as a flexible multi-purpose structure and has been a common design feature of urban centers in Eastern Europe since the 1960s. Transforming the module into a café and deli met the challenge of combining a minimal interior with the maximum use of space. The result is a unique place to enjoy homemade Finnish snacks and Neapolitan coffee. The hovering cube with rounded corners and a glossy surface is located in a Berlin courtyard, where its radiant color contrasts the surrounding neo-classical façades ●

B

KIOSKI BERLIN

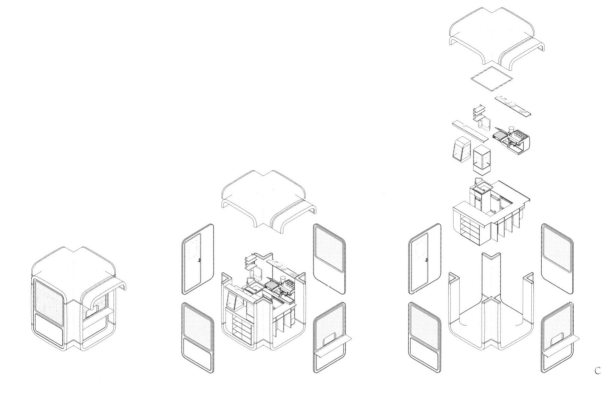

C

D

E

Architect **DONGQI DESIGN**

Location **CHANGZHOU — CHINA**

Year of Completion **2018** Gross floor area/seats **288M2/74**

A

B

A  material detail
B  interior overview
C  dining area
D  detail of curved bars
E  floor plan
F  juice bar

Designed by dongqi Design and located in Changzhou, China, C.F. Café reveals a cheerful and modest branding character by spatial redefinition and material selection. The concept introduces the idea of an open market space, where areas for bakery, coffee, and juice making are redefined by using three curved bar counters respectively. The used materials show a mixed character of modernity and tradition. Three quarters of the bar tops are made of stainless steel, while the rest – including the side of the counter – is made of terrazzo and exposed aggregate. Above the bar counters three curved caps, incorporated into the ceiling, highlight each area. The counters merge into the wall and create the concaved stainless-steel walls for showcase. The inner façade incorporates terrazzo bar tables and transparent glass. The entrance, curving inward, echoes the curved elements of the space and welcomes the people come forth ●

C.F. CAFÉ

C

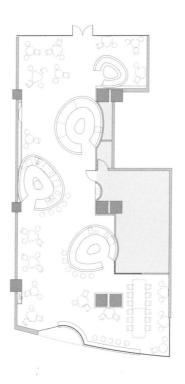

D E F

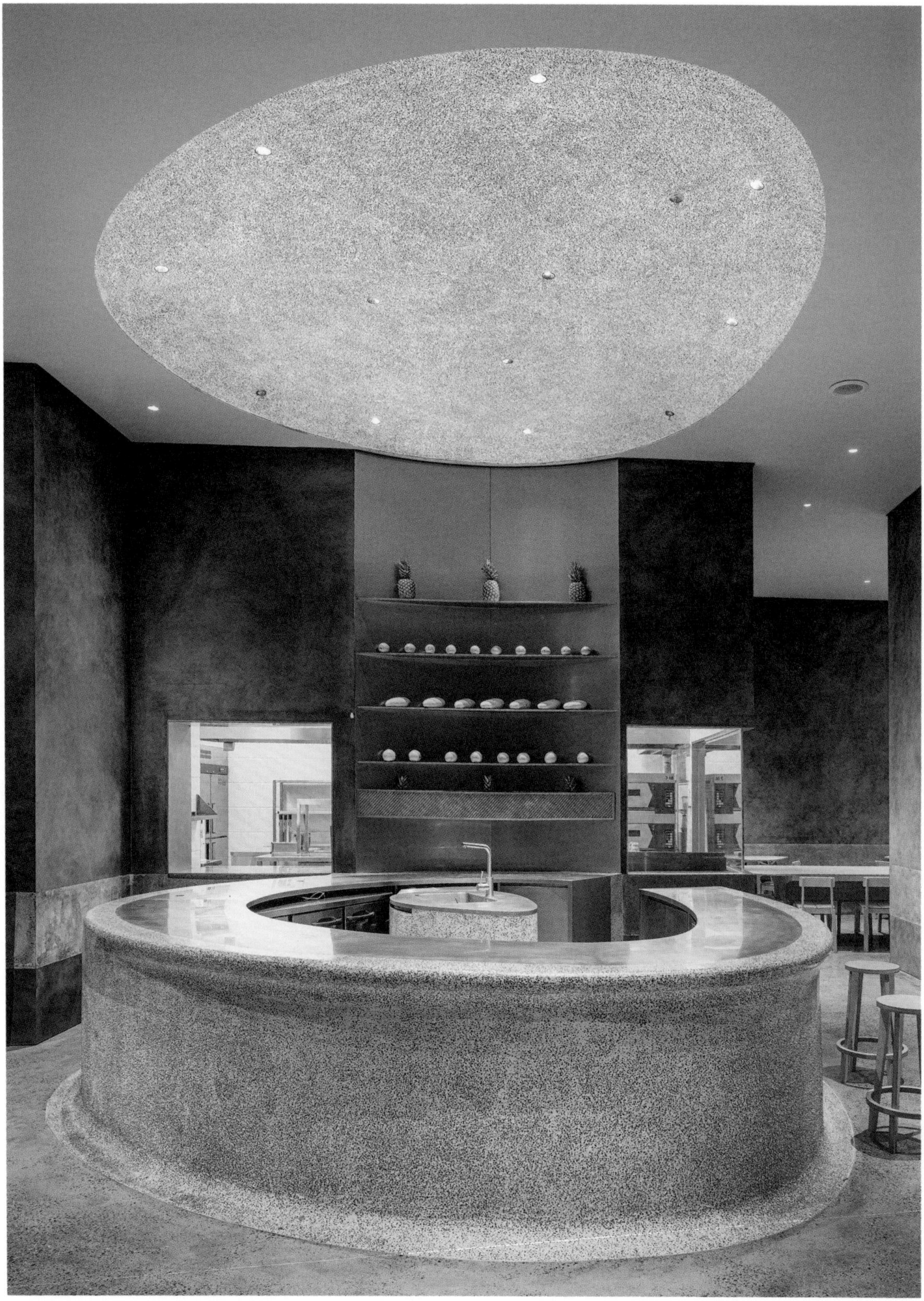

A

Architect **STUDIO AKKERHUIS**

Location **AMSTERDAM —
THE NETHERLANDS**

Year of Completion **2021**  Gross floor area/seats **310M2/125**

A unique place where there is always something going on, where people can enjoy the good things in life, and where everyone is invited to have experiences: This is the idea Studio Akkerhuis developed together with the owner of Lebkov & Sons for the new brand identity. In continuity with their existing cafés, the new location is conceived as a kitchen/living space where customers and baristas share the same table or counter designed for them to rest, enjoy a meal, as well as prepare good coffee.

The bar and the open kitchen form the centerpiece that organizes and structures the entire café space. The seating areas, articulated around the central bar, are designed to create a diversity of interesting spaces throughout the different areas of the café. These include wooden benches along the wall to the right, a snake-like, concrete shared table along the façade, the central bar counter, flexible furniture, with seats and tables in the back, and a wood podium with cushions and small tables.

The close interaction between customer and barista is emphasized by the low glass showcase, which offers a transparency through space and better visibility of the products. This sharing principle is also represented by the Lebkov pattern where black squares mix with light squares. Previously realized with small tiles, the pattern has been reinvented using an innovative material called Wood-Skin. This new material is made up of wooden panels with engraved patterns that give organic shapes to the covered objects. The iconic Lebkov pattern can be found at a different scale in the open storage where fresh products and coffee beans are displayed in a modular steel structure. The shelves and boxes of this storage are realized by folded Wood-Skin square modules that can be freely placed into the steel frames. The wood, concrete, and steel, combined with a discreet lighting design radiate warmth, authenticity, and unity. The mix of materials creates a welcoming environment, a truly special place for everyone to enjoy ●

LEBKOV & SONS CAFÉ

B

D

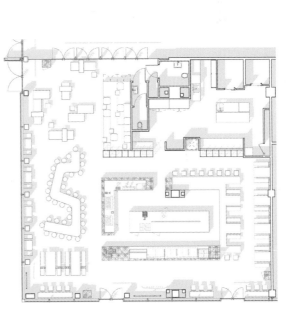

E

LEBKOV & SONS CAFÉ

Architect **VO TRONG NGHIA ARCHITECTS**

Location **VINH — VIETNAM**

Year of Completion **2018** Gross floor area/seats **687M2/199**

A

Nocenco Cafe is located on the last floor and rooftop of a seven-floor concrete building. From these heights the guests have a view over the center of Vinh city in north-central Vietnam. The architects created a unique and attractive addition to the building by covering the existing structure with bamboo material, which expresses the project's essence of lightness, and is easy to access in this tropical climate. There are ten bamboo columns to hide the concrete structure as well as four additional columns. They elegantly divide the lower floor into different private areas. The cave-like space can never be fully experienced but every spot has a view to the surrounding city. While the dome and rectangular volumes on the rooftop fit in the existing L-shaped space, pedestrians can recognize the bamboo covered ceiling from the street. On the rooftop, a club was created as a gathering space for all inhabitants of Vinh city ●

NOCENCO CAFE

B

C

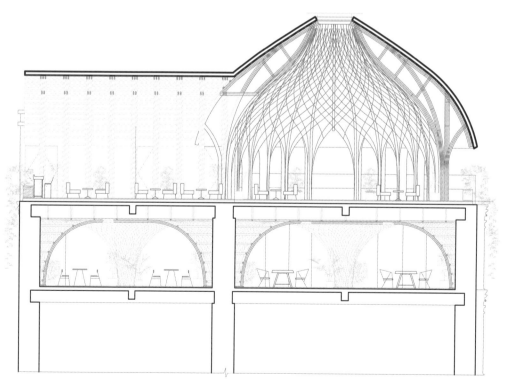

D    E

NOCENCO CAFE

A

Architect PONOMARENKO BUREAU

Location KHARKIV — UKRAINE

Year of Completion 2021  Gross floor area/seats 86M2/38

B

A  general view
B  counter
C  modular furniture
D  floor plan
E  view from entrance zone
   towards the metal wall
   with rainbow zinc coating
F  detail of furniture and
   plants

23a is a city coffee shop that is located on one of the historical streets of Kharkiv near the Kharkiv Theater of Opera and Ballet. During the daytime, it is a coffee shop with craft drinks, light meals, and desserts, but in the evening it turns into a party place with wine and a bar ambiance. The place is divided into different zones: a table for a big company, an adaptive central zone, and the entrance zone. Furniture is modular so it can easily be rebuilt according to the function of a space. The most essential adaptive elements are tables and benches that help visually change the space and plants. The key element is metal, processed with a rainbow zinc coating, which creates a unique effect with the light and materials. It was challenging to find a suitable coating, so after a large number of experiments, architect Volodymyr Ponomarenko chose film as coverage ●

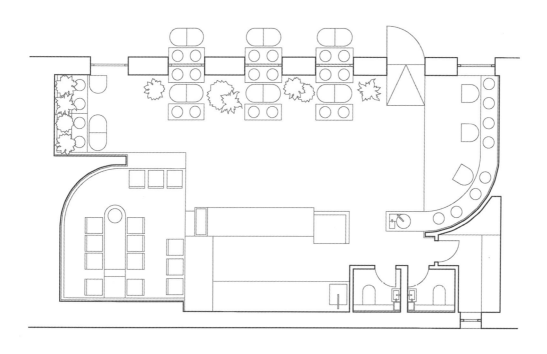

D

E   F

| | |
|---|---|
| Architect | **STUDIO VOS** |
| Location | **BERLIN — GERMANY** |
| Year of Completion | **2017** Gross floor area/seats **134,5M2/28** |

A

B

A quick coffee at the
counter
B wood wool panel acoustic
wall, stage, and flexible
area
C waiting benches rescued
from swimming pool
in Wedding
D counter and waiting room
E floor plan
F room divider to the
kitchen

Mirage is a French bistro at the Nettelbeck-
platz in Berlin Wedding. It was founded and
largely implemented by three friends: two
Germans and one Frenchman, all of whom
live in Wedding themselves. The Mirage is
not only a café and bar, but also a meeting
place for artists and creative people, with
concerts, readings, exhibitions and workshops. In addition to developing a suitable
spatial concept, the task was also to integrate the furniture and equipment that was
already partially available. While drawing up
the execution planning, it was particularly
important to take into account that the clients were able to build everything themselves. The result is a light-flooded room with
a central counter and a small stage, whose
background — geometrically shimmering
wood wool panels — is acoustically effective.
The harmonious mix of concrete, wood,
bright colors, and many plants make Mirage
an inviting and cheerful place ●

MIRAGE BISTROT

MIRAGE BISTROT

BARFUSSGANG

D

E

F

MIRAGE BISTROT

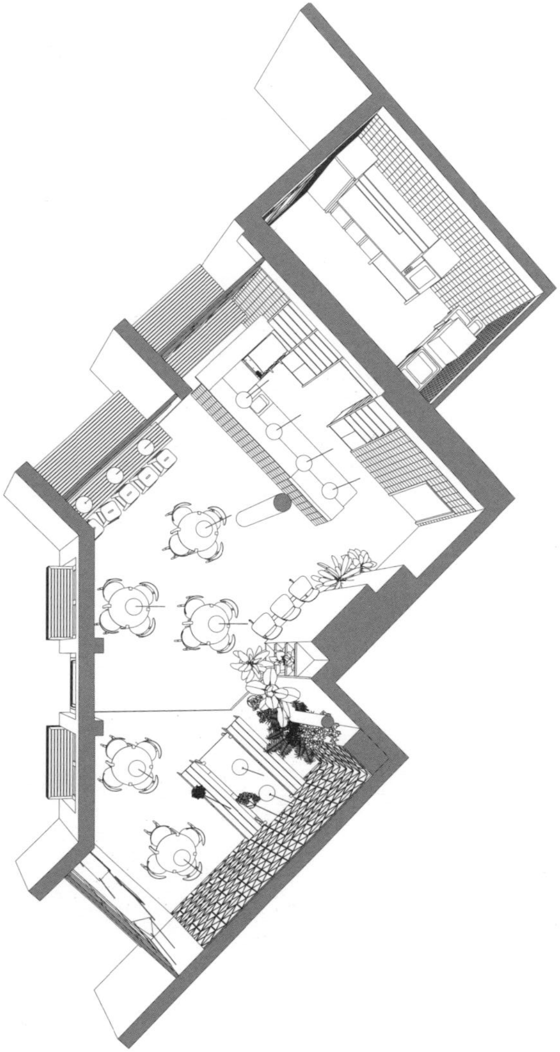

A

Architect **ARK4LAB OF ARCHITECTURE**

Location **KAVALA — GREECE**

Year of Completion **2017** Gross floor area/seats **130M2/50**

B

A seating area with portrait made of traditional tiles
B view from outside
C bar counter with copper wall
D wooden platform
E floor plan
F sitting area with terrazzo floor and rhinoceros model

Black Drop coffee shop is located in Kavala, a city in northern Greece. The office ark4lab cooperated with bonos construction to transform a stand built of mosaic into an interactive space for exchanging views on the art of coffee. Materials such as copper, terrazzo, exposed concrete, old wood surfaces, and rusted walls give the customer the impression of being part of a laboratory, where one can act and react. Among the old walls are artworks by kuki design, embedded in the space, such as a portrait made of traditional tiles and a rhinoceros model interpreted in triangles. A wooden platform built in levels and positioned towards the Kapnergaton Square removes the coffee shop's boundaries with the exterior, transforming it into an urban space of gathering. This is where post-industrial, contemporary, urban esthetic meets the obsession of coffee lovers ●

BLACK DROP

C

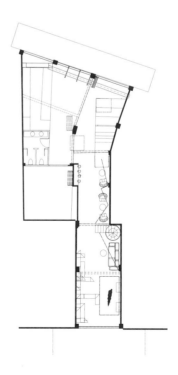

D E　　　F

BLACK DROP

Architect **STUDIO SHOO**

Location **YOSHKAR-OLA — RUSSIA**

Year of Completion **2021** Gross floor area/seats **100M2/48**

A

Muka & Fartuk is a cozy café and shop that offers a wide choice of breads, pastries, cakes, and puff pastries. The concept of the interior was inspired by close-ups of the textures of artisan bread – mesmerizing lines along which the bread cracked, a crispy crust, and the milky white color of the flesh.

The interior space was divided into two zones with a wall that has arches in the form of bread loaves. At the entrance there is a space for a quick snack. A room with a cozy, low-seating area was designed with a round table for companies and a comfortable soft sofa. The walls are finished with silk textured plaster, while the pieces of furniture were created by the architects specifically for this project. With warm tones of plaster, smooth surfaces of furniture as well as rough walls, and terrazzo they created a play of textures, factures, colors, and tactile sensations ●

MUKA & FARTUK

B

C

D

E

A

Architect **ATELIER MEARC**

Location **SHANGHAI — CHINA**

Year of Completion **2018**   Gross floor area/seats **188M2/24**

B

A façade
B arch wall
C floor plan
D coffee salon
E coffee bar with counter
  made of bookshelfs

Longshang Books Cafe combines book, coffee, and salon and each function interacts with the other two. Therefore, a kind of arch wall was applied by atelier mearc. The element has been adopted in the spacious coffee area and bookshelf structures. Especially in the latter experience, sitting in the arch wall reading, or browsing along the bookshelf backside becomes an interesting examination of this delicate correlation of people and environment. There are 20,000 books and 24 coffee seats in this 188-square-meter space. Both the cold-natured stainless steel panel and the warm and natural featured wood materials are used throughout the café. Most basic, familiar materials are connected in an unfamiliar way, so they change their original nature. This change, light and heavy, enhances the abstractness of the space that leads to a wonderful experience ●

LONGSHANG BOOKS CAFE

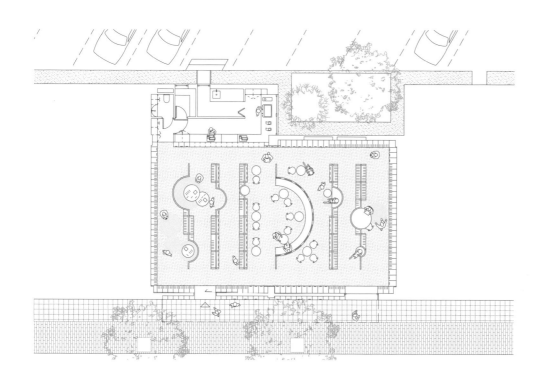

C

D

E

LONGSHANG BOOKS CAFE

# JUST ANOTHER CUP

# A COFFEE TODAY

Around 2.25 billion cups of coffee are drunk worldwide every day, an average of just a quarter of a cup per capita: however, over 30 percent is consumed in Europe, and over 20 percent in Asia and Oceania. In Africa, on the other hand, the figure is just seven percent, and in Central America only 3.5 percent. Northern Europeans lead the way: Finland, the Netherlands and Sweden consume nine to ten kilos of coffee per capita and year, followed by Denmark and Norway. Germany, for example, consumes only 6.65 kilos per capita, but with an average annual consumption of around 168 liters, it has long since become a country of coffee drinkers – beer only accounts for just under 95 liters. At the same time, most adults can also meet here for a coffee, as 76 percent consume coffee regularly. Water, on the other hand, is drunk regularly by only 62 percent, and beer by 36 percent. So people meet for a coffee, or another and another. And people meet in the coffee house. And not only because the beverage is prepared by dedicated professionals – a craft that is almost a science in itself – but also because this is a space that welcomes a diverse range of social actions. This is a place to meet one's friends, enjoy the atmosphere, to take a break while shopping, to think about the working day ahead, to plan the next place to visit on a tour of the city, to read the paper or a book. Cafés and coffee houses also serve as neutral ground to meet prospective clients.

What is happening at the other tables or the throngs of people passing by offer a wealth of entertainment and plenty to talk about, which is why cafés have evolved over the years to become multipurpose city locations. One feels at home, the room functions as a private space away from the everyday hustle and bustle. These are places where "just five minutes" can morph into hours. Hours where one can simply refill what was supposed to have been "just one cup". The type of coffee doesn't matter, whether filter coffee, mocca, dopio, frappé – there are countless national and international ways to consume this beverage. With or without sugar, with diverse alcoholic additions, with milk or froth, coffee cream or simply eked out with water. While wine is composed from around 400 different

aromas, coffee has more than 800. Everyone has their own favorite ways of enjoying a good cup of coffee!

Since the 1990s the focus was again on the quality of coffee with exquisite Arabicas and finest espresso drinks conquering the mainstream. The era also witnessed the birth of coffee shops that paved the way and initiated a kind of "Starbucksization". Cafés with carefully selected ambiances spread the vibes of New York even to the remotest small towns. Coffee lounges turned into the new home offices and hubs of business meetings. The paths of the third wave of coffee from the 1990s to today also go back to the roots, back to the character and the original taste of the bean. What once became a practically packaged product and was then sweetened and available to go as the symbol of a cosmopolitan lifestyle, is now a luxury food in the same category as wine, it is the beginning of a renewed appreciation of the "black gold". Transparency is quintessential of the third wave movement, starting with the direct contact of roasting companies and dealers with the farmers, via the guaranteed sustainable cultivation of the coffee berries, up to sufficient pay for a decent standard of living for all involved. Here, direct trade is the new fair trade. But how sustainable is "fair" coffee? The answer is up to each and every one of us. Through the way we set

Italian-American café in New York City, USA

our priorities when choosing the way we buy our beans, the coffee culture, and perhaps the world somewhat too, can be made a little better – regardless of whether we prefer the taste of Arabica or Robusta.

In good coffee shops, the barista knows everything about it and gladly passes on his knowledge to the guests. He is the bartender – in Italian barista – but also the sommelier of the bean drink, knows not only the origin and refinement of its raw material but also all conceivable craft preparations and coffee mixed drinks: be it with milk froth or with alcohol. While in Italy baristas actually fulfill the functions of barkeepers and are in charge of the preparation and serving of all types of drinks, in other countries baristas are almost exclusively associated with the art of coffee preparation. Baristas are true masters of this art, which has by now become a science of its own. This is because a coffee drink, whether classically filtered or decorated artistically, is only as good as the skill of the person preparing it. The Coffee Diploma System of the Specialty Coffee Association of Europe, SCAE, is an internationally recognized certificate and a possibility of paving the way of young professionals. There are six different skill areas – introduction to coffee, green coffee, sensory skills, roasting, brewing and barista skills – in which the future baristas are trained and examined after which they can officially call themselves approved and qualified. But this is not the end of the road. Professional training courses as a roaster, buyer, instructor, or the step to opening one's own café with a roasting facility offer opportunities for further development, self-fulfillment, and professional advancement. Or one can become a coffee sommelier; the person with in-depth knowledge and understanding of the composition of the product itself.

Thus, from the coffee farmer to the barista, many specialists are involved until the perfect cup – or the perfect glass – is served to us in the coffee shop. And we enjoy their work in very different atmospheres, in rooms that are as diverse and lovingly designed as the beverage itself.

A

Architect **ARCHITEKTEN: FELIPE PALACIOS + JOHANN MOELLER**

Location **QUITO – ECUADOR**

Year of Completion **2020** Gross floor area/seats **80M2/18**

Coffee Shop QTGC is a renovation project of an underused space within the Quito Tennis and Golf Club, one of the most prestigious private clubs in Ecuador. The design proposal consisted of a hybrid space shared between two programs: a contemporary cafeteria and a small gallery. To achieve this, Architekten reinvigorated the usage of the space through design, and generated a versatile environment to enjoy coffee and art while maintaining the feeling of spaciousness. The cafeteria is structured in three subzones: booths, lounge, and preparation counters. The lounge expands into a double height, while the booths are contained in a wooden loop. The application of materials like French oak wood contributes to the warmth and continuity of the space.

The choreography of materials includes the contrast between navy-blue armchairs, large quartz counters, and a diversity of furniture fabricated by Teknomueble. The seating niches were designed in detail, considering the user's ergonomics and comfort. Facing the lack of natural lighting, Cimsa used backlit, stretch-fabric Barrisol panels that resemble an overhead light entry. The entrance doors feature a sliding system that enables a complete integration between the entrance hall and the coffee lounge when open to the public. In addition, the door´s design incorporates openings that guarantee adequate ventilation once the space is closed. The gallery, on the other hand, is an open space that serves as a multipurpose room. It is distinguished by a skylight that brings natural homogenous light and helps release hot air ●

COFFEE SHOP QTGC

B

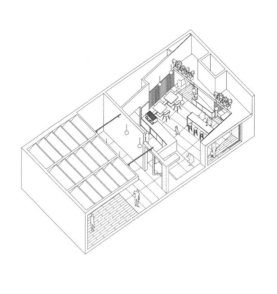

C

D  E

F

Architect **GIORGIO GULLOTTA ARCHITEKTEN**

Location **HAMBURG — GERMANY**

Year of Completion **2017**    Gross floor area/seats **80M2/6**

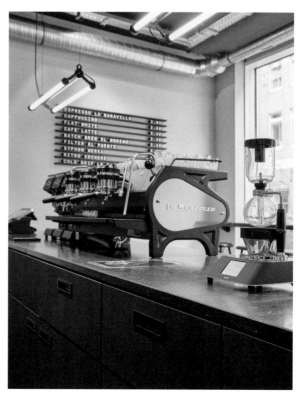

A

B

A counter back side
B frontal view with zones of light and dark tones
C general view
D counter with a Belgian bluestone surface and brass pilaster strips
E floor plan
F glass, stone, brass, and light contrasting each other

Located in the immediate vicinity of the Hamburg City Hall, the new concept store of the Elbgold coffee roasting company opened in December 2017. Under the name Coffee Lab, very special ways of preparing coffee are presented here. Coffee is brewed classically, with hand filters, Aeropress, or Syphon. In addition, there are Cold Drip and freshly tapped Nitro Brew. During the so-called cuppings, several coffees are tasted side by side to show how manifold they can be. The focal point of the space is a nearly 6.5-meter-long counter with a Belgian bluestone surface and brass accents. Shell limestone in Roman bond was chosen for the back wall. The pared-down and understated color scheme, cold-drip brew shelf, and nitro vessels create the desired laboratory character. The pendant lights, visible ventilation pipes, and maxite flooring support the industrial character of the interior. The material mix of natural stones and metal creates a classy but cool look and forms the atmospheric basis ●

ELBGOLD

C

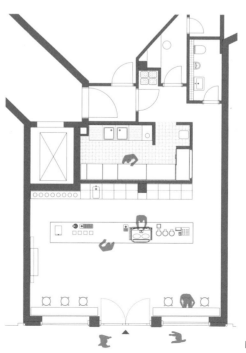

D E                    F

A

Architect PARTY / SPACE / DESIGN SC

Location KRABI — THAILAND

Year of Completion 2021  Gross floor area/seats 300M2/100

B

MUCH & MELLOW

A view from pastry to
   coffee shop
B façade at twilight
C homemade bread baking
D seats in wooden setting
E floor plan
F warehouse look at the
   coffee bar

The brief was to renovate the new restaurant located at the basement of the Family tree hotel to three sections: restaurant, a coffee shop, and a pastry shop. All three areas are managed by the same family, but each member has different competencies. The challenge was to present these three areas in the same mood and tone. the design concept started with the ideas of a tree (like the name of the hotel) around which people live together in very different constellations and constitutions. This results in a design that connects all the rooms and these moods and tones.although all three areas are also interconnected, each has its own seating area, but also encourages customers to take a stroll through the space as a whole ●

C

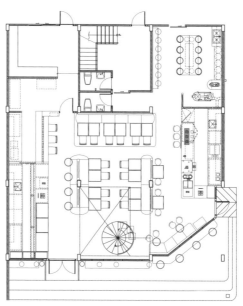

D  E

F

MUCH & MELLOW

Architect CARLO RATTI ASSOCIATI

Location LONDON — UNITED KINGDOM

Year of Completion 2021  Gross floor area/seats 350M2/25

A

B

A lower part of the counter
   built with coffee ground
B the extra-deep circular
   counter with brass surface
C the café space prioritizes
   safety and sociality using
   bactericide materials
D Italian coffee served in
   post-pandemic social life
E floor plan

Designed by international design and inno-
vation office CRA – Carlo Ratti Associati,
Caffetteria constitutes a substantial area at
leading coffee brand Lavazza's flagship store
in London. The original design concept by
CRA is conceived as a social proximity café
that promotes a collective coffee experience
in a safe manner. The research led by CRA inspired the ultimate selection of lamps, which
possess disinfecting properties to remove
bacteria and viruses on the countertop. Co-
inciding with this is the extensive use of
brass, a germicidal material, which is used
throughout the shared surfaces of the café,
such as the counter top. Moreover, the lower
part of the counter is built using coffee
ground to reflect the principles of circular
design. Its convex shape, which at one meter
of depth is wider than usual, allows customers and employees to interact safely. The
number of seats is not fixed since they can be
reconfigured easily as a part of the design ●

CAFFETTERIA

D

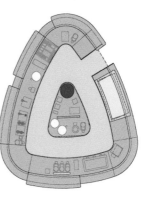

E

CAFFETTERIA

A

Architect  NOTA ARCHITECTS
Location  BEIJING — CHINA
Year of Completion  2018  Gross floor area/seats  221M2/80

B

A spatial sequence of the
  Plank Path with Water
  Surface, Floating Hut, and
  Ship Deck Garden
B mist-covered water stage
  for baristas
C main volume invites to
  look at the skyline
D axonometry of the
  Floating Hut
E Floating Hut transparent
  to the surroundings while
  reflecting them

Seesaw Coffee is located in a bookstore on the top level of Chaoyang Joycity mall in Beijing. In response to the context, the design offers a visual language of diverse sceneries by making use of the existing floor height difference, creating a sunken plaza: Plank Path – Water Surface – Floating Hut – Ship Deck Garden. Stepping down from the bookstore onto the plank path and passing by the coffee bar and sales display, one enters the seating area, as if walking from the path into the water, and then onto the sunken deck. Blocks of wood and planters, customized at high and low levels altogether form an outdoor garden, which coincides with the surrounding landscape, while offering different options to take over the space. Sizes and rhythms are carefully considered to encourage uses of multiple target groups and social scenarios regarding comfort and a sense of security ●

SEESAW COFFEE

D

E

SEESAW COFFEE

| | |
|---|---|
| Architect | STUDIO 211 |
| Location | ESSLINGEN AM NECKAR — GERMANY |
| Year of Completion | 2018    Gross floor area/seats    97M2/25 |

A

B

A counter area
B general view of the café
  and lounge area
C view through the café
  towards the lounge area
D floor plan
E lounge area

This daytime café is divided into three zones. The first area at the entrance is the barista zone with a spacious counter as an eye-catcher. It is flooded with light and offers the possibility to enjoy your espresso directly at the bar or to sit at the window. The monolithic counter made of shaped tiles characterizes this space and leads into the second zone of the self-service café with a classic seating area. The third room behind it already appears somewhat darker due to the smaller windows and has been converted into a lounge area. Low tables, armchairs, and a fitted bench invite to a cozy coffee or cocktail. Wooden and golden tones dominate this area and make the light seem warmer. All three zones are connected by a green linoleum floor and round, sound-absorbing ceiling elements with indirect light ●

CAFÉ KAUZ

C

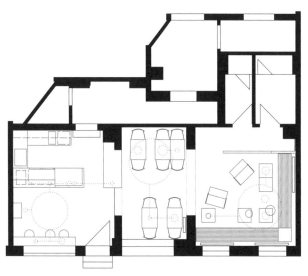

D

E

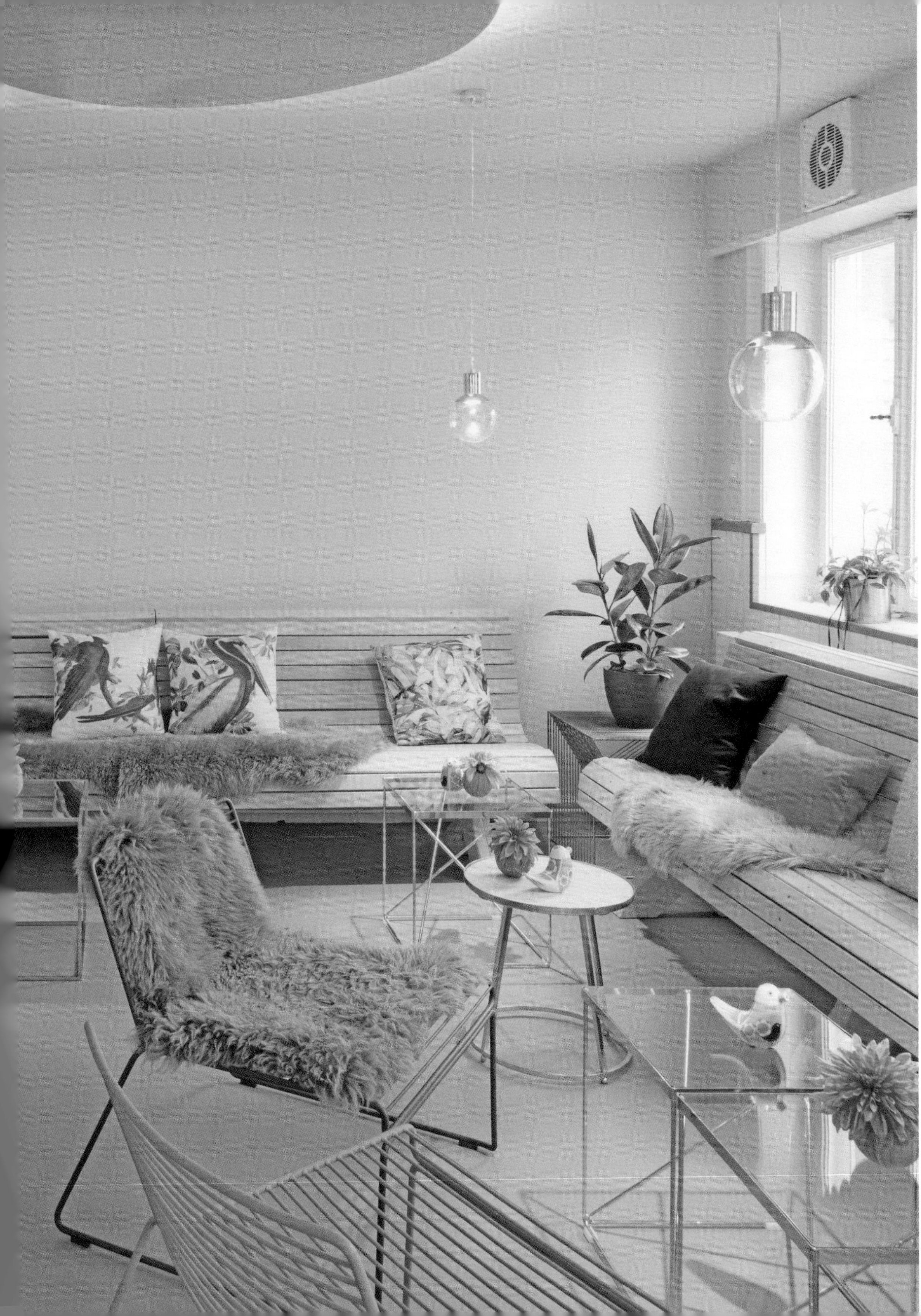

A

Architect ABERJA

Location FRANKFURT / MAIN —
GERMANY

Year of Completion 2021    Gross floor area/seats 50M2/12

B

A side wall with zig-zag
shapes
B large mirror surface with
water-like texture behind
the bar
C furniture and circular light
sculpture on the ceiling
D scenographically staged
bar
E floor plan

This italo-american bar reflects Italian lightness. Large reflective surfaces with a water-
like texture on the ceiling and rear wall bring
in light and significantly enlarge the room.
The side walls are clad with custom inlays
made with copper, cherry wood, and fabric,
which have a chic, eclectic quality. They enhance the effect of the metallic surfaces and
catch the attention of passersby. The place-
ment and form of the bar and other pieces of
furniture are highly scenographically staged
and use space in a manner that enhances the
feeling of the drama brought upon by the
other surfaces. Warm, pulsating tones, finishing that contrasts with the materials of the
walls, and zig-zag shapes that echo themselves at different scales are all set off by indirect ceiling-directed lighting that reflects
off a variety of surfaces ●

BAR AMERICANO

D

E

BAR AMERICANO

A

Architect **JON ELIASON DESIGN STUDIO**

Location **STOCKHOLM — SWEDEN**

Year of Completion **2018** Gross floor area/seats **180M2/120**

At the first visit, the architect was already fascinated by this beautiful space and wanted to preserve its unique identity but add the coffee. What would happen if one does fill the volume of a room with coffee? A horizontal line runs through the rooms aligning with the height of the espresso machines. Underneath that line everything gets a dark coffee tone, while above the room stays in its original condition. For Johan & Nyström Odenplan, Jon Eliason Design Studio has created the interior design, special designed lamps and sofas, and a system with connectable cushions. Visiting the Johan & Nyström on Hantverkargatan, Odenplan or Swedenborgsgatan, one should pay attention to the coffee cups, designed by the architects as well as the oblique line representing the angle at which the barista spins the coffee in the cup ●

JOHAN & NYSTRÖM

B

c

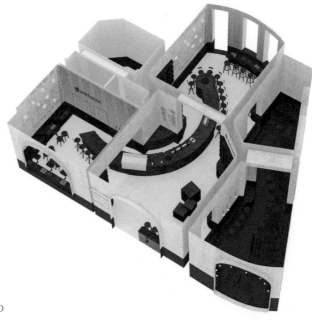

D

E

JOHAN & NYSTRÖM

A

Architect **DONGQI DESIGN**

Location **SHANGHAI — CHINA**

Year of Completion **2020**  Gross floor area/seats **200M2/56**

The Basdban, designed by dongqi Design, is located on the first floor of a historical building in Shanghai that has lived through several renovations. The design is supported by the close collaboration of the brand founder, baristas, roasters, graphic designers, structural engineers, constructors, and the dongqi team. They aim to create a comprehensive space accommodating coffee, roasting, retail, and event functions.

The architects carefully selected and preserved the traces left by ages of renovations. Customized stainless steel was used as the main material for the newly built part. Meanwhile, six-millimeter-thick, horizontal steel plates run though the entire location, merging the new design with the old building in a restrained manner. The rectangular space in the middle is defined as a flexible, multi-functional area that allows dining, events or other uses. A stainless-steel rail system is introduced to highlight the boundaries of the area. These rails are symmetrically distributed along the columns and beams, accommodating functions such as lighting, monitoring, and metal curtains that divide different areas.

The massive, eight-meter-long floating bar counter is integrated in the original structure of the building. It gives customers a direct view of the baristas' work. At the same time, dongqi echoes the graphic design of this project to express the quirkiness of Basdban, which also means "super good" in Sichuan dialect. At the façade, a 12-meter-long stainless-steel sliding door was incorporated while respecting the texture of the building. The result of this project's design is a restrained interpretation of the bold and rebellious brand spirit ●

B

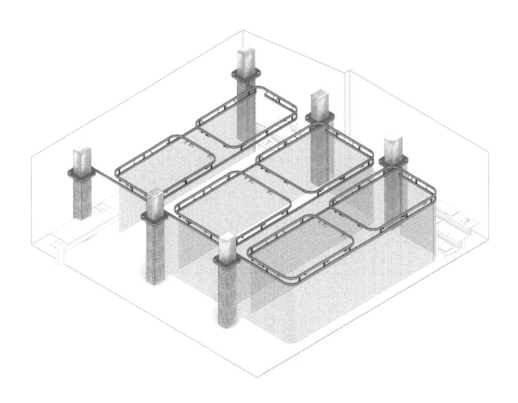

C

D  E

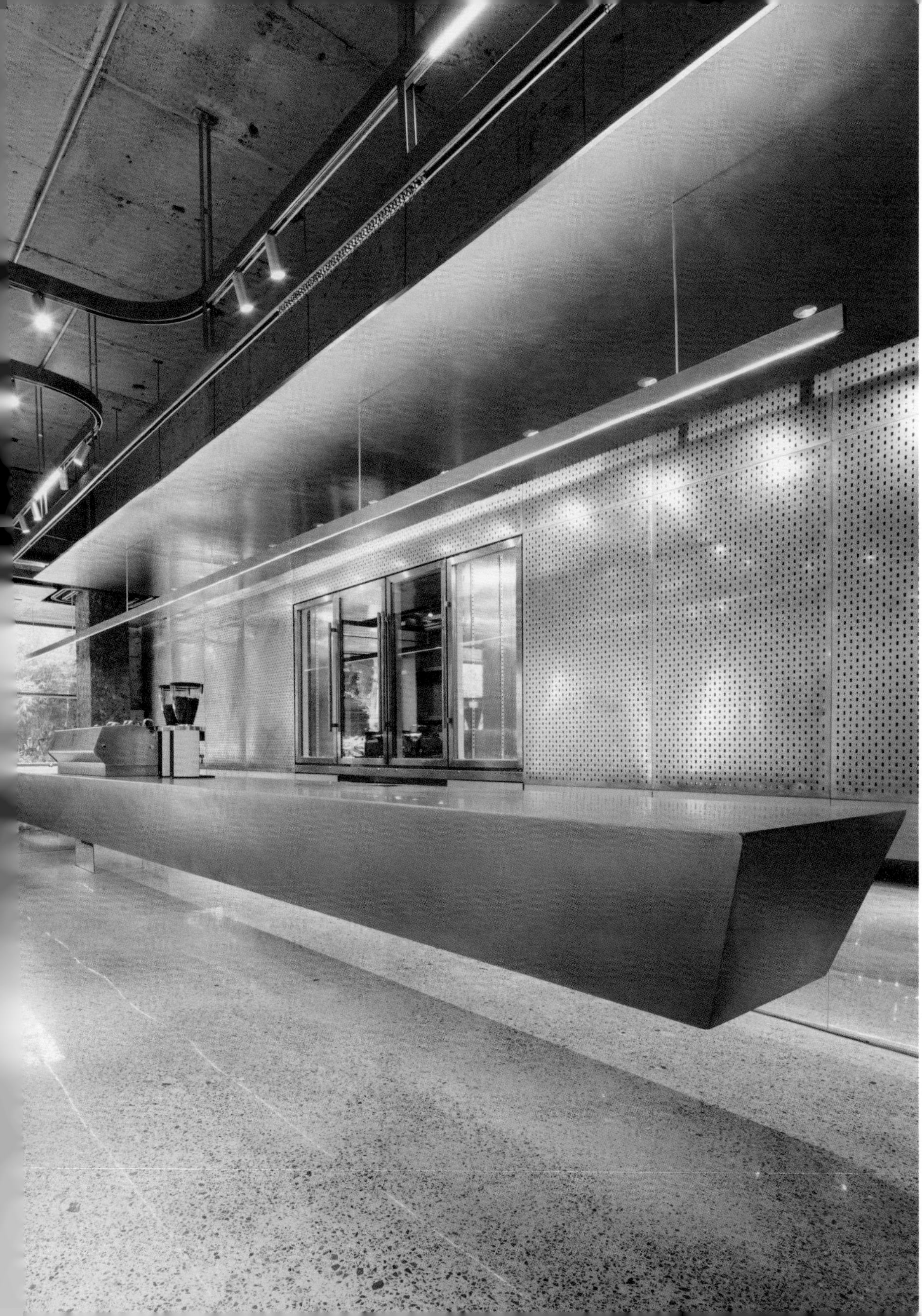

A

Architect  MV STUDIO

Location  SAN JUAN — PUERTO RICO

Year of Completion  2018  Gross floor area/seats  120M2/40

B

Gustos Coffee was created in terminal B at San Juan airport in the wake of hurricane Maria that passed over the island of Puerto Rico in September 2017 and destroyed the previous retail space. A chevron-patterned, medium-toned, cladded wall greets you as you enter the space. The same cladding was carried to the ceiling to add warmth. Perspective lines draw the eyes to the back of the space. At the center, two oversized communal industrial farm tables take the stage under rows of industrial fresnel lights with barn door shutters. There is a beautiful relationship between a pair of contrasting materials: raw stock matte-black steel channels and a refined, marble appearance, sintered stone. Brass metal highlights on the wall sconces in the booths and in hardware throughout shine proudly in their dark surroundings ●

GUSTOS TERMINAL B

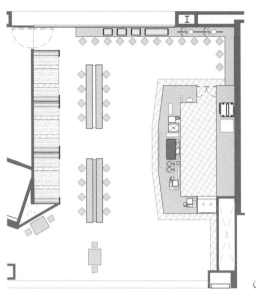

C  D

E

F

| | |
|---|---|
| Architect | # BUREAU EUGENIE ARLT |
| Location | # VIENNA — AUSTRIA |
| Year of Completion | 2019 |
| Gross floor area/seats | 75M2/8 |

A

B

A exterior with garden
B view through the opened
  window front
C floor plan
D seating area connecting
  inside and outside
E baked goods and
  beverages being offered
F counter cladded with
  green tiles

The Austrian bakery chain Felzl aims for a respectful and responsible handling of regional products and for the avoidance of food waste. It's branch in the second district of Vienna was designed by Bureau Eugenie Arlt and creates an esthetically reduced, yet friendly atmosphere. The location focuses on the bakery trade, displayed by the central mono block counter cladded with green three-dimensional tiles from Italy. The tiles pick up the chain's corporate identity color and complement the oak floor and wooden furniture. The architects furthermore incorporated stools by Thonet and lights by Gubi, Molto Luce as well as &Tradition. The café's window front can be fully opened towards the neighboring market. This allows the spaces of interior and garden to be perceived as a unit ●

BÄCKEREI FELZL

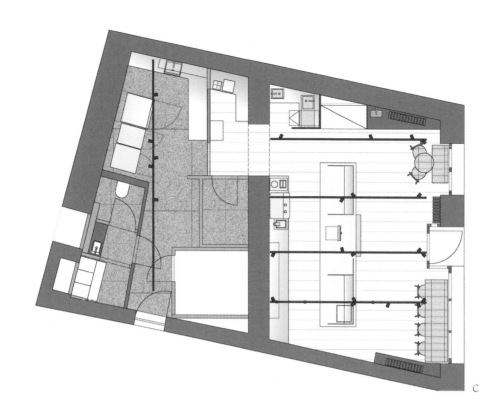

C

D E

BÄCKEREI FELZL

# FROM HEPBURN
# TO JARMUSCH

# COFFEE
# IN CINEMA

"I drink a lot of coffee before I go to sleep so I can dream faster" – with shaking hands, actors Steven Wright and Roberto Benigni consume an unhealthy amount of espresso and cigarettes, while talking about the benefits of coffee and that there should be caffeine popsicles for children. What seems like an absurd discussion, is just one of eleven short stories from Jim Jarmusch's anthology film "Coffee and Cigarettes" (2003), the title representing the common thread that connects the episodes. This ode to simple conversation is shot in black and white and thereby invokes a nostalgic atmosphere, a reminiscence to iconic times of film history. In fact, the relationship of cinema and coffee goes back to the very beginning: On the 28th of December 1895, the world's first commercial film screening took place at the Grand Café in Paris. It was held by the Lumière brothers, featuring their groundbreaking invention, the Cinématographe, as well as their first films, which showed scenes of everyday life in France. Early cinema thrilled its audiences with its overwhelming realism, that, at the same time, seemed like a product of magic. To satisfy the demand for this new medium, further coffee houses were transformed into picture palaces at the beginning of the 20th century.

To this day, the dream factory of cinema has continued to infuse peoples' lives with magical stories, while casually incorporating the mundane element of coffee. One of them is Jean-Pierre Jeunet's „The Fabulous Destiny of Amélie Poulain" (2001). Amélie, a whimsical young woman, uses her vivid imagination to secretely improve the lives of the people around her, while not being able to escape her own loneliness. The shy waitress works at the actually existing Parisian Café des Deux Moulins, where she meets Nino and starts to pursuit her own happiness. In Jean-Luc Godard's „2 or 3 Things I Know About Her" (1967), the coffee shop serves as a space for philosophical thoughts. While filming a cup of coffee from above, the camera zooms in until the black liquid and the ripples of stirring fill the entire screen, resembling a galaxy in space. A calm voice-over reflects on the essence of existence and communication, while the images occasionally retreat to the coffee shop surroundings, drawing the audience

Café des Deux Moulins in
Paris, France

ESSAY

back into everyday reality. An endearingly mundane Katherine Hepburn is shown in George Stevens' „Woman of the Year" (1942), in which she plays a modern-minded correspondent who falls in love with a sports reporter. To demonstrate her abilities as a house-wife, she wants to prepare breakfast for her husband. While still wearing her fur coat, Hebpurn cluelessly ends up brewing a bubbling, muddy mess of a coffee. Another iconic female character is Holly Golightly in Blake Edwards' „Breakfast at Tiffany's" (1961). The opening scene, showing Audrey Hepburn in a black dress and pearls, gazing into the window of the famous jeweler while having a croissant and take-away coffee, was cemented in film history. The way in which a cup of coffee can have crucial effects on the story of the film has also been shown in Alfred Hitchcock's „Notorious" (1946), in which Ingrid Bergman gets poisoned by cof-fee, as well as in Bryan Singer's „The Usual Suspect" (1995), where a broken coffee mug reveals the true identity of a criminal mastermind. In Michael Mann's „Heat" (1995), Robert De Niro and Al Pacino sit down for a coffee in a quiet yet suspenseful showdown be-tween master criminal and obsessive detective. While having their first shared screentime, the two acting gi-ants casually discuss their characters' careers, women and lifestyle philosophies.

film poster of „Notorious" (1946)

Audrey Hepburn behind the scenes of "Breakfast at Tiffany's" (1961)

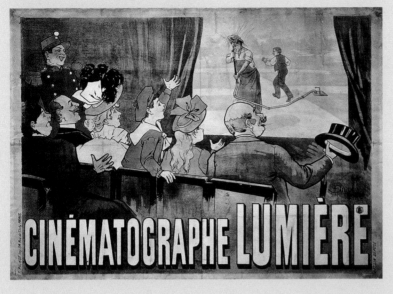

Marcellin Auzolle's
advertising poster for the
Cinématographe Lumière

The element of coffee has been permeating many periods in film history dripping through virtually every genre. It can also be found as the subject itself in Marc James Francis' documentary „Black Gold" (2006), which portraits the efforts of an Ethiopian coffee union manager travelling the world in the attempt to obtain a better price for his workers' coffee beans. The coffee house as an integral location has also found its way into the ever growing category of Japanese anime. In the world of Studio Pierrot's series „Tokyo Ghoul" (2014), creatures that can only survive by devouring humans live among society in secrecy, hiding their true nature in order to survive. Since water and coffee are the only ordinary groceries they can digest, a small neighborhood café serves as a central place of retreat. Entering the realm of TV shows, one can not neglect the lasting effect of David Crane's and Marta Kauffman's popular sitcom „Friends" (1994-2004), in which the main characters frequently visit a New York City coffee house throughout the series. There, they spend much of their free time discussing the trials and tribulations of modern city life implying that there's nothing a cup of hot coffee with your friends can't fix.

A

Architect **PIERCE DESIGN**

Location **SEATTLE, WA — USA**

Year of Completion **2019**    Gross floor area/seats **123M2/41**

B

A outdoor at dusk
B barista serving coffee at
  the slow bar
C floor plan
D gold ceiling and tropical
  wallpaper at the back
  corridor
E leather, steel and marble
  bar detail
F entry scene at the pastry
  case and espresso bar

Santo Coffee asked Pierce Design to create a visually unique and modern space using a material palette that would be inspired by their Columbian roots, but not nostalgic. The result: An approachable, luxurious café that respects and displays the craftsmanship of the barista. Dark color tones and tactile materials are used in a stripped down concentrated form. Highlights of gold and tropical prints punctuate the inner volumes of the space. Leather tames blackened steel, monolithic marble is juxtaposed with concrete, and textured, undulating walls flow beneath the ceiling above. A continuous ribbon of wood flows from bar to bench, filling the storefront window. Every detail has been thoughtfully considered, creating a rich experience for both coffee connoisseurs and the greater community ●

SANTO COFFEE

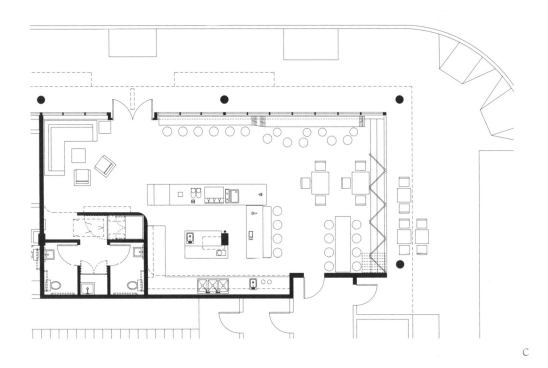

C

D E                F

SANTO COFFEE

A

Architect **FROMME & BLUM**

Location **POTSDAM — GERMANY**

Year of Completion **2017**   Gross floor area/seats **200M2/45**

A view from the counter into a part of the guest room
B stove bench with colorful tiles
C stage with lounger swings
D planning as 3D model
E view towards exit

The Rathaus pharmacy, a relic of the 1990s, has become a meeting place with a café, bistro and bar. Here you can find Italian coffee from the best scouts in town, seasonal cuisine, regional beer, exhibitions, readings, concerts, and gossip from Babelsberg. The interior – a combination of historic old stock and new design elements – can be experienced in a new way from every perspective. Historic charm meets maritime pine, floral wall panels and the Sweet Samurai bar stool also designed by Fromme & Blum. The Kellermann, Babelsberg, deliberately conveys the improvised character of a living room and is intended to give the operators room to unfold, because the design allows it to be independently adapted, changed and optimized at any time and again ●

KELLERMANN

B

C

D

E

KELLERMANN

| | |
|---|---|
| Architect | PARTY / SPACE / DESIGN SC |
| Location | BANKOK — THAILAND |
| Year of Completion | 2021 |
| Gross floor area/seats | 150M2/50 |

A

Bod-Kod-Chong cafe is located in the Plumeria House, a unique designed building by Thai cosmetic brand Mistine, inspired by the white plumeria flower which is the brands iconic symbol. The interior design had to blend both brands' concepts and designs beginning with an interpretation of plumeria flowers. The brief was to seek for something simple and suitably in depth for the clients.

The layout adopts the flow of coffee brewing, emphasising a concept of layers to design each area in the coffee shop. A spiral staircase without a pillar in the middle of the coffee shop represents a shape of flower petals as well as pouring liquids. A circular ceiling that rotates in the café mimics the plumeria blossom, reminding guests that they are in Plumeria House ●

BOD-KOD-CHONG

B

C D

E                                                                                          F

BOD-KOD-CHONG

A

Architect  I IN

Location  OSAKA — JAPAN

Year of Completion  2021    Gross floor area/seats  345M2/49

Since this is the first coffee shop by the brand to open in a new region, the interior design of the Blue Bottle Coffee Umeda Chayamachi Cafe had to consider the message of Blue Bottle Coffee conveying a story, easy to understand for the customers. The iconic blue logo that suddenly appears in the city scape, and the joy of discovering the familiar blue of the brand are expressed using various lights and materials.

On the ground floor, the customer is surrounded by the essence of warm wood, a big drip station filled with bright, welcoming light, and a stage-like space where the barista making coffee stands out the most. The counter made of hairline, polished stainless steel radiates a dignified presence. The surface reflects the scenery of the space, softening the boundary between the barista and customers. The special blue glass used Throughout the store, expresses the brand's iconic character with its unique transparency.

At the staircase area, a glass chandelier hung from the ceiling spreads throughout the atrium. Coffee-colored, spherical glass, made by the glass artist Fresco based in Osaka, gently welcomes guests. Customers can feel the flow of an impressive view of light and color with the three-dimensional space experience of the stairs. In the center of the first floor, mainly surrounded by white-colored materials, a special area stimulates the five senses of the visitors. By spending time here, while bathing in the images and sounds that seem to fall from the ceiling, guests are offered a special experience that can change the impression of time. Images and music, created in collaboration with Panoramatiks, allow the customers to fully reset themselves. The bench made of a special material employs a mechanism that only the person who actually sits can feel through a sensory experience. It is not just a concept, but a place that really stimulates the five human senses. The space has transformed into a completely new café interior, that offers a special experience while enjoying a cup of coffee ●

B

C

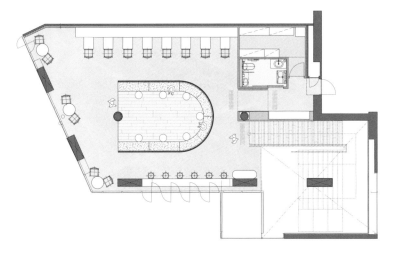

D

E

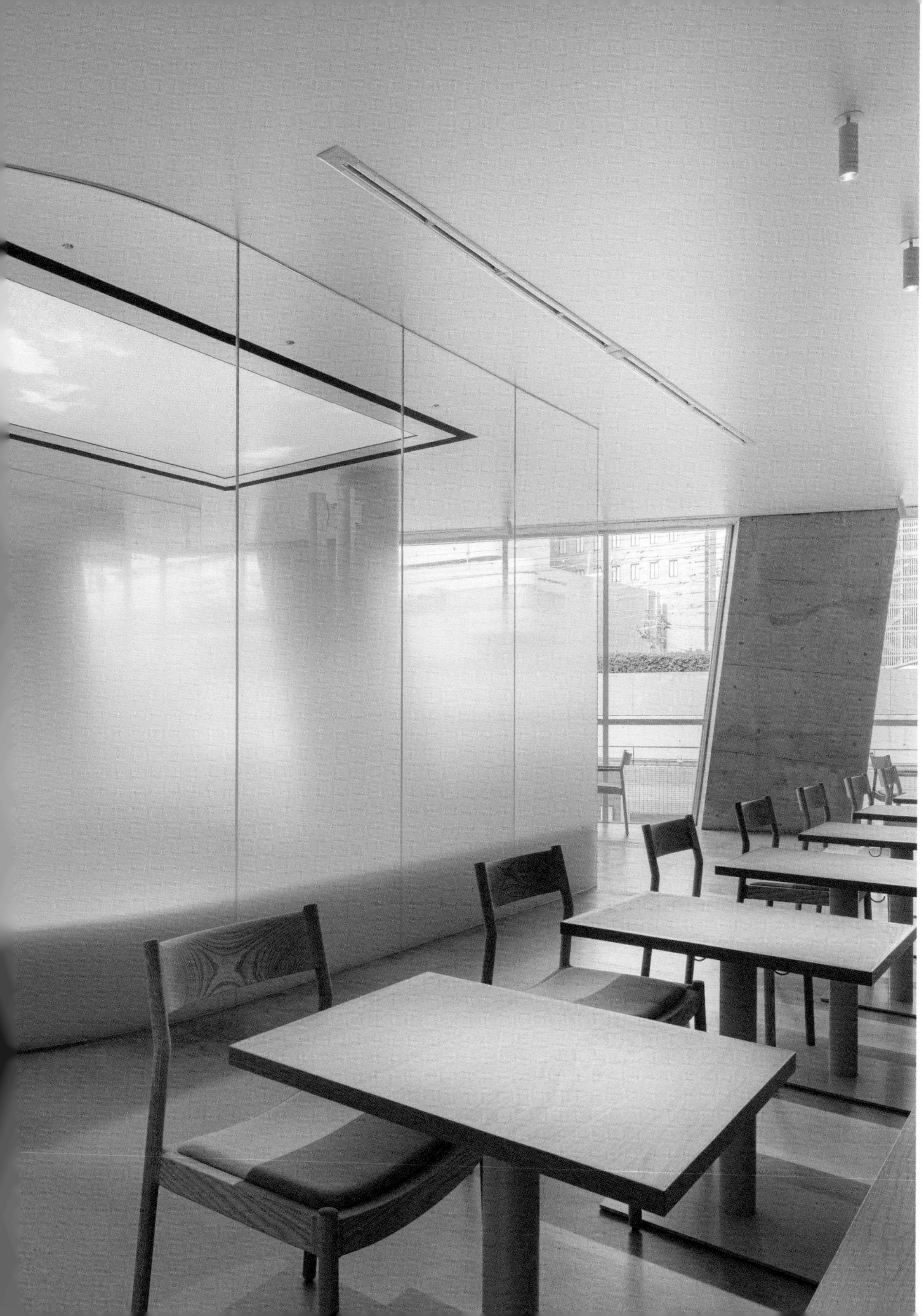

A

Architect  NONESPACE

Location  GIMPO-SI — SOUTH KOREA

Year of Completion  2021  Gross floor area/seats  170M2/60

B

A general view with timber
   interior
B detail
C brick-structure of piggy
   three in the cellar
D straw walls of piggy one
E ground and first floor plan
F blue furniture

SECOND PIGGY HOUSE

The design of this café refers to the story
"The Three Little Pigs" known since the edition of English Fairy Tales by Joseph Jacobs
in 1890. The fable tells about three pigs who
build three houses of different materials: A
Big Bad Wolf blows down the houses made
of straw and sticks but not the one made of
bricks. In nonespace's version the second
piggy already wins because log houses can't
be blown away either, but can be realized
with less work. The second pig thus has the
best work-life-balance and the third forgets
about the brick structure. It builds a log
house as well.

   The aged log of the outer layer represents the warm image of houses from the
fairy tales of our childhood and embraces the
surrounding nature with a subtle atmosphere. Nonespace created a çozy mountain
lodge by using the same internal finishing ●

C

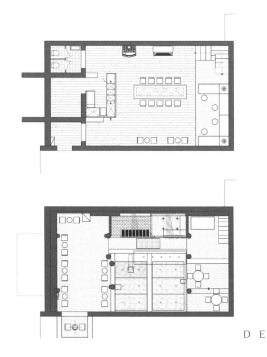

D E

F

SECOND PIGGY HOUSE

| | |
|---|---|
| Architect | KONRAD KNOBLAUCH |
| Location | HAMBURG — GERMANY |
| Year of Completion | 2020 |
| Gross floor area/seats | 40M2/18 |

A

B

A view of the massive stone
counter from the entrance
B detail of stone counter
and menu in oak frame
C floor plan
D room concept and seating
E view into the café from
the retail area

On the second floor of the Alsterhaus in Hamburg, the crème de la crème of menswear is lined up next to each other. In the middle of it all one finds the Echt.Zeit Café. Furnished with genuine marble stone, black steel, oak wood, and selected upholstery fabrics, the small café offers seating away from the hustle and bustle of the shopping mall. Everyone will find their favorite spot here, whether at the bar stools at the counter in front of the rounded façade overlooking Jungfernstieg and Alster, on the upholstered bench or the comfortable wooden chairs. The café in the Alsterhaus is the flagship of the Echt.Zeit coffee house chain. Guests can expect a special greeting from its southern German home: Lake Constance wine from the Kress winery, whiskey from the Senft distillery, and special coffee in collaboration with Merchant & Friends ●

ECHT.ZEIT CAFÉ

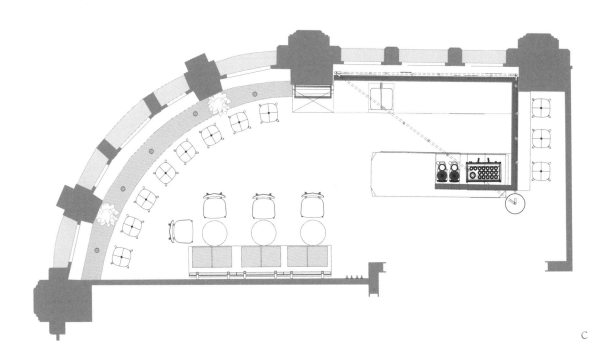

C

D    E

ECHT.ZEIT CAFÉ

A

Architect DIRSCHL.FEDERLE
_ARCHITEKTEN
Interior Designer DIANE BÖHRINGER
Location FRANKFURT/MAIN —
GERMANY Year of Completion 2016
Gross floor area/seats 310M2/75

B

CAFÉ LIEBIEGHAUS

A column and cross ribbed
  vaults
B furniture from the villa's
  inventory
C room with a library
D entry with seating area
E floor plan
F room with a fireplace

This popular café is located at the Liebieg-haus in Frankfurt/Main, a museum of sculpture situated in a late 19th-century historicism villa near the Main river. In the course of the building's ongoing renovation the architects dirschl+federle worked with interior designer Diane Böhringer to refurbish and expand the café. They renewed the technical construction and the surfaces while compiling the furniture from the inventory of the house. By displaying a collage of stylistic elements they reflect and complement the building's own history, which includes different European building styles. Some of the numerous historical features are the wooden paneling, the column, and the cross ribbed vaults. Apart from the main café the garden and entry, as well as separate rooms with a fireplace and library, invite to an extended visit ●

C D

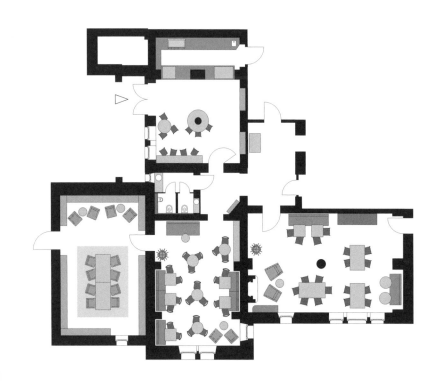

E F

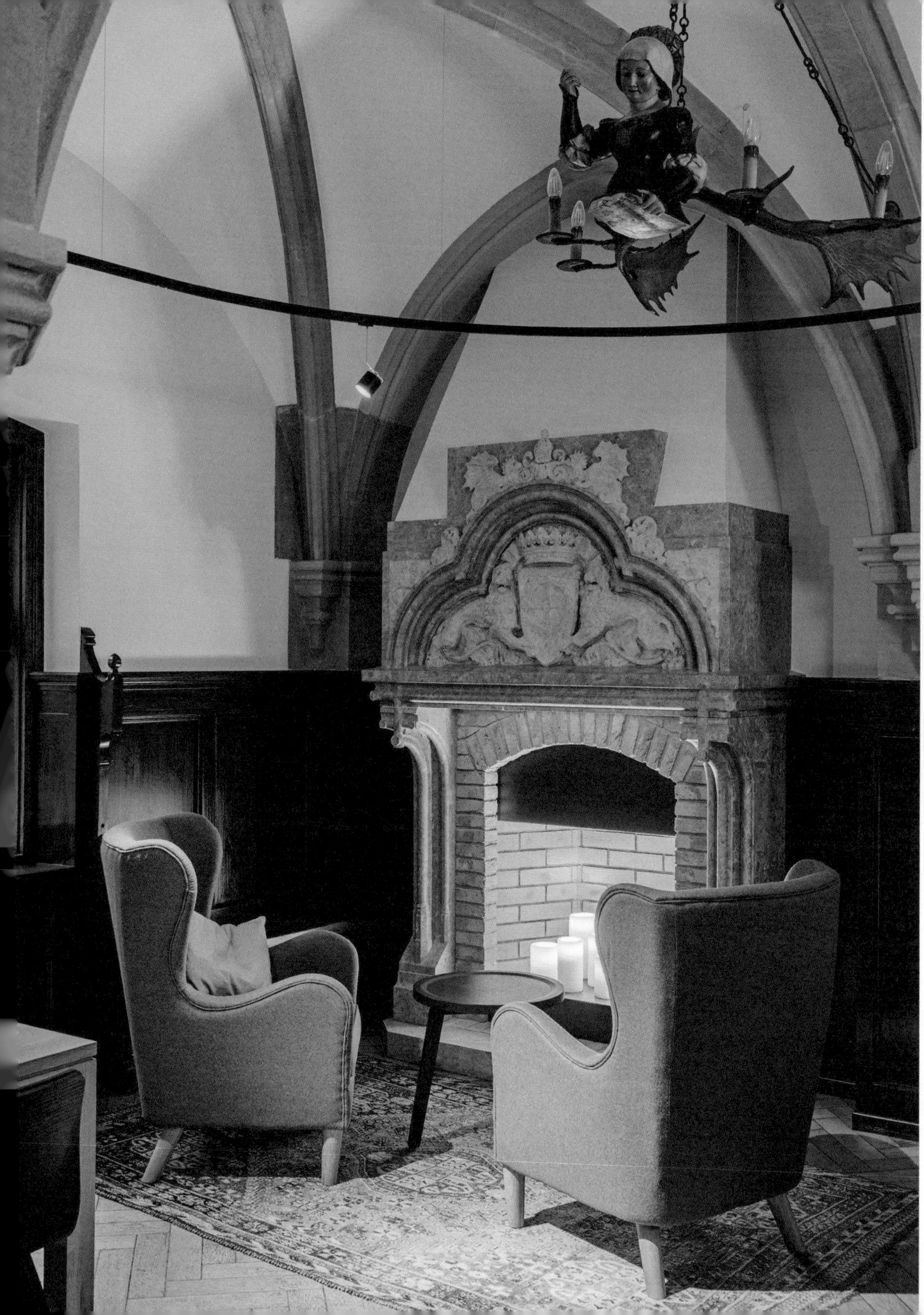

A

Architect IPPOLITO FLEITZ GROUP —
IDENTITY ARCHITECTS
Location MUNICH — GERMANY
Year of Completion 2019 Gross floor area/seats 64M2/45

The Schwabing district of Munich is well-known for its vibrant street life by day and by night. Young people in particular love the cozy atmosphere the district has to offer. Within this setting, the architects have realised a café/bar concept for New Era Coffee, which unites the lifestyle factors of enjoyment and taking time.

The value of a good cup of coffee lies in its complex flavors, which only properly unfold when temperature and pressure are correctly applied during the making process. The interior design translates this guiding principle into a space that condenses a diversity of people within a common lifestyle. Professional workshops, just one part of New Era Coffee's diverse offering, underscore the brand concept of a new era of enjoyment. This era begins with its own premises in the heart of the city, after already having been successful with mobile offerings at festivals and street parties. Thanks to a clever interior design, the café/bar, with its informal atmosphere, offers the perfect setting for all tastes at any time of the day or night. Different seating situations are grouped around a central counter, forming separate zones, highlighted by the special design of floor and ceiling. A small, elevated niche from which one can overlook the entire space, is designed as a room within a room, so that the flowing overall effect is not impaired by partitions. In combination with high-quality materials and a supporting light design, the focus is on the warmth of the coffee during the day. In the evening, the mood shifts to the coolness of a stylish drink.

Despite the limited space available, a café/bar has been created, in which not only regular customers feel at home, but also walk-in customers, who are quick to spy the inviting oasis of coziness through the glass façade. New Era Coffee's confident policy of only using organically grown beans from selected regional roasters is the special reward that awaits anyone who steps inside – a value that is now also reflected in the brand image ●

NEW ERA COFFEE & BAR

B

C

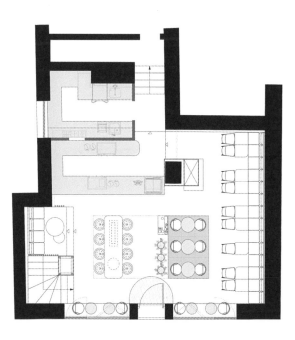

D    E

NEW ERA COFFEE & BAR

A

Gustos SCA – Academia del Café is a space with very clean lines and understated beauty where the materiality and design elements did not become an unnecessary distraction for the students. In addition to limiting the visual noise, the overall intent was to show the many facets of Gustos Coffee Company. Any customer can experience the coffee shop, the SCA facility, and, through the steel and glass window from within the SCA space, a view of their roasting facilities. A lot of the references that are used for the space and material choices were derived from the original esthetic of the adjacent coffee shop, which also assumes a relatively clean, pristine design. That continuity helped create a seamless transition from the Gustos Coffee Shop into the SCA facility ●

B

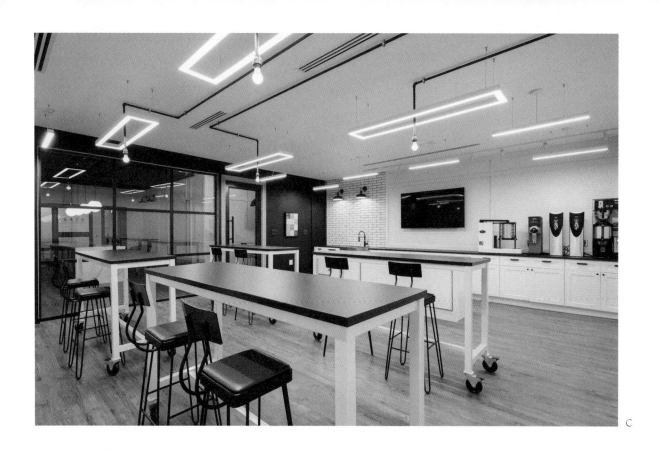

C

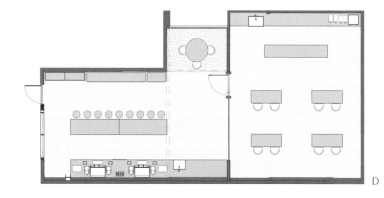

D

E

A

Architect **DONGQI DESIGN**

Location **NANJING — CHINA**

Year of Completion **2018** Gross floor area/seats **70M2/20**

The new UNiUNi Coffee Shop in Nanjing, China, was designed by dongqi Design and has been dedicating to coffee retailing as well as coffee culture preaching. Moreover, the UNiUNi team earned a high reputation in the World Barista Championship. In this spirit, the architects developed the idea of a stage and backstage. The curved bar counters are set like stages on the side where the baristas brew coffee, while the customers watch the making process from every corner of the space, just like the audience. The experience of buying, tasting, and making can take place simultaneously, in any of the four counters of the space. The bar tables are suspended from to the ceiling by using stainless steel tubes, connecting to each other by hinge joints. The vertical steel tubes are connected two by two, hinged to horizontal steel tubes at a height of three meters above the ground. They help integrate and stabilize the whole structure. The shelves are also hung from steel tubes along with all the facilities, machines, and fridges, hung from the tabletop by using L-shaped steel bars. Water is supplied inward from the ceiling and drained upward by using pumps in the steel tubes. Everything is attached to the ceiling, including power strips. The exposed pipes, wires, and equipment enhance the experience of the backstage concept. Curved steel sheets and clear glass are the main elements of the façade. Red LED lights project the gradient patterns of the steel sheets, casting fading shadows on the white steel panels and the top. The narrow red steel frame outlines the main entrance door, echoing the elegant and exquisite, while moderating the attitude of the design, as well as the brand spirit ●

UNIUNI COFFEE SHOP

B

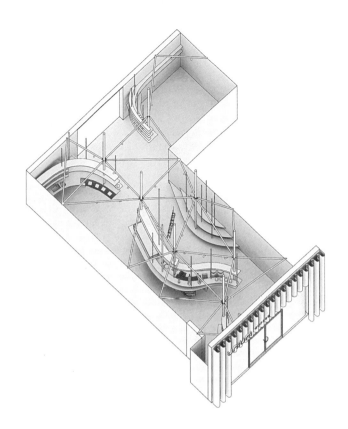

C

D E

F

UNIUNI COFFEE SHOP

A

Architect IFUB*

Location VIENNA — AUSTRIA

Year of Completion 2019    Gross floor area/seats 134M2/32

The new Café Kandl in Kandlgasse 12 of the 7th district is a contemporary Viennese coffee house: timeless and yet exciting, a family-friendly café with delicious breakfasts and lunches by day, and an outstanding cocktail bar at night.

With its oak parquet floor and matching ash paneling and furniture, the main seating area is inspired by the classic coffee houses. The graphic patterns of the wood, in combination with the colored fabric of the curtains and upholstery, brings the necessary freshness to a well-established concept. The wood paneling design was derived from the new Café Kandl logo, and is not only visually appealing but also directs to the exits and the sanitary rooms. Encircling the main entrance, a curtain of thick yellow fabric protects against wind and noise from the outside. The color and material concept of the main seating area uses warm colors for a cozy flair. Special attention was paid to durability, value, and feel, as well as the use of real materials. For the freestanding furniture, oak-topped tables were custom made, with legs from ash and feet in galvanized steel. The stackable chairs — also in ash — were made by a Finnish manufacturer and fit perfectly into the overall design.

At 15:30 the bright and friendly café-restaurant turns into a cool cocktail bar. The dark-red curtains behind the bar are drawn, and at the same time the lights are dimmed and set to a color that invokes the evening atmosphere. In combination with the green marble the heavy red curtain creates a perfect stage for the bartenders and their drinks. Behind the bar the square pattern in the parquet transforms into black and white concentric circles. Gleaming stainless steel and sparkling galvanized steel complete the picture.

Since the first COVID-19-lockdown, the service has been switched to fine dining in the evening and Café Kandl is no longer open during the day hours ●

CAFÉ KANDL

B

D

E

A

Architect  LE HOUSE

Location  HAI PHONG CITY — VIETNAM

Year of Completion  2017  Gross floor area/seats  1,000M2/180

B

A view from the first stair case looking towards the atrium full of trees
B panoramic building façade
C ground floor towards the middle garden
D top floor garden looking at the greenhouse block with atrium
E diagram
F entrance hall
G view down to the atrium with curved staircase made from rust-painted steel and a curved concrete bench

The No.1986 Coffee & Restaurant with its trend-setting design, tells a very special story. The design of the lobby refers to the "Mo Qua" scarf – a Vietnamese kerchief in the shape of the crow's mouth – which is popular known as Northern girl's wearing. The front of the building is made from natural materials. Inside, the large space opens up over several floors, connected by two blocks of special long stairs to the so-called "Paradise". The No.1986 Coffee & Restaurant appears like a quiet garden with sunshine falling through the roof shaped like a scarf and surrounded by old brick walls. The furniture and decoration stand apart from these walls, but share the industrial style. Greenery, spreading out on all floors, provides a homogeneous and calm look and feel●

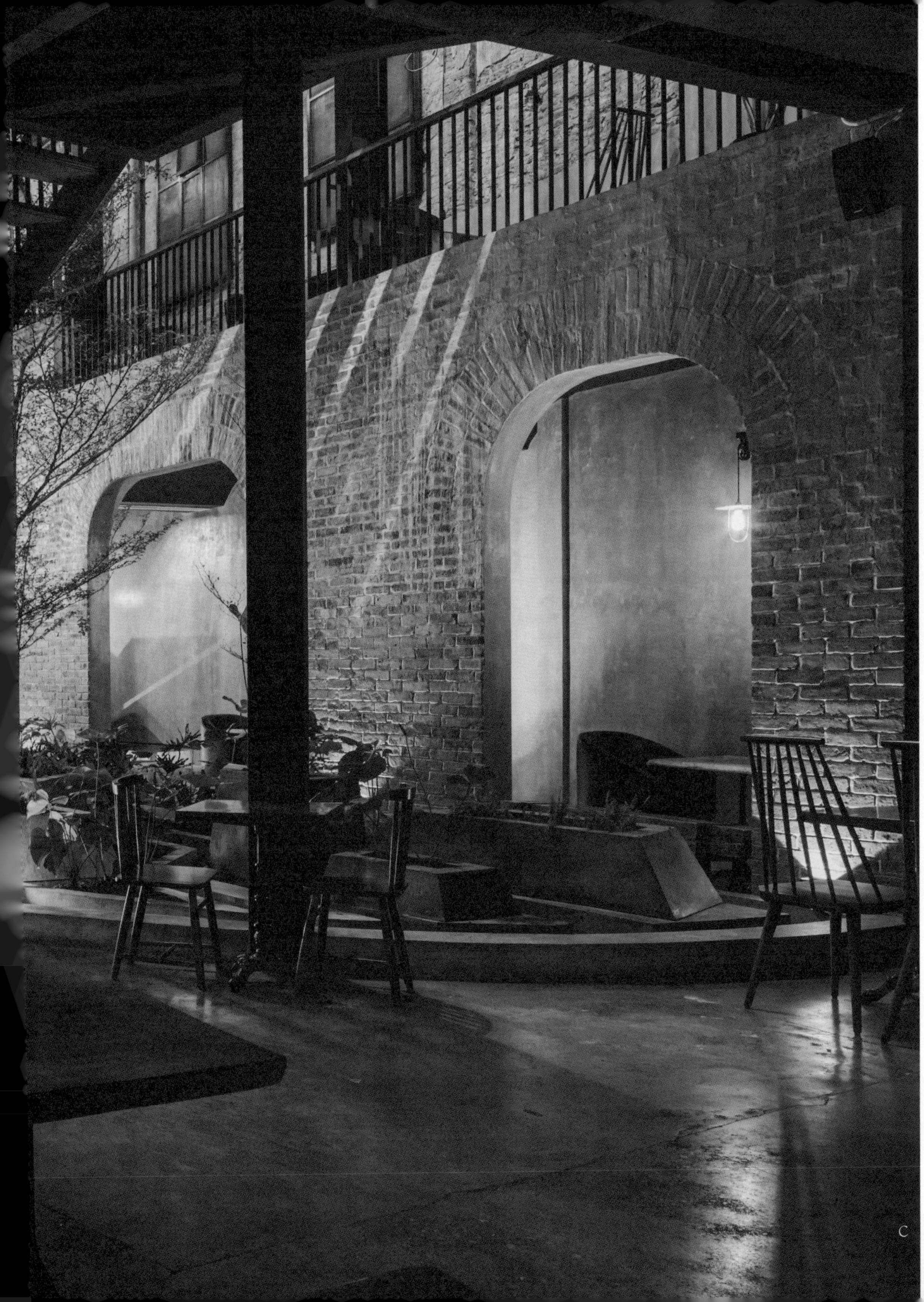
C

D

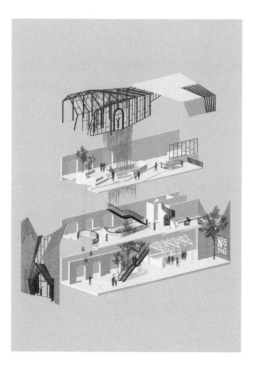

E F G

# CAFÉS BY LOCATION

# ARCHITECTS & DESIGNERS

# PICTURE CREDITS

ALEJANDRO A.
MARIN GAOS
www.alejmarinphoto.com
156 — 159

SORIN MORAR
www.sorinmorar.de
208 — 211

MICHELE
NASTASI
www.michelenastasi.com
72 — 75

HIROYUKI OKI
HCMC
212 — 217

IVÁN ORTIZ
www.parfotografos.com/-
ivan-fotografia-arquitectura/
56 — 61

JI-HOON PARK
Seoul
184 — 187

TOM PARKER
www.tomparkerphotography.com
132, 133

PARTY / SPACE /
DESIGN SC
www.partyspacedesign.com
32 — 35, 128 — 131, 176 — 179

JEREMY
PEARSON
CC-0 / commons.wikimedia.org
164

JENS PFISTERER
www.jenspfisterer.de
188 — 191

BRIAN
PREDSTRUP
www.agentevers.se
148 — 151

QIAN SHIYUN
137, 139

PAOLA
QUEVEDO
SANTOS
www.pquevedos.com
200 — 203

ROBERT RIEGER
www.robrie.com
20 — 23

RKO RADIO
PICTURES INC.
CC-0 / commons.wikimedia.org
166

MARTIN RUGE
VON LÖW
www.martinruge.de
77

DAVID SANCHO
大衛
CC-BY-3.0 / commons.wikimedia.org
52

JUNG-BAE SHIN
Seoul
44 — 47

ANDREW
STOREY
www.lightcatcherimagery.com
168 — 171

JOCHEN
STÜBER
www.jochenstueber.de
124 — 127

STUDIO 211
www.studio-211.de
140 — 143

TRIEU CHIEN
88 — 91

NIKOS
VAVDINOUDIS,
CHRISTOS
DIMITRIOU
www.studiovd.gr
104 — 107

REINHOLD
VÖLKEL
CC-0 / commons.wikimedia.org
55

NICKY WEBB
www.nickywebb.at
68 — 71, 160 — 163

WU QINGSHAN
80 — 83

SAÚL
YUNCOXAR
www.outervision.xyz
36 — 39

# IMPRINT

The Deutsche Nationalbibliothek lists this
publication in the Deutsche Nationalbibliografie;
detailed bibliographic data are available on
the Internet at http://dnb.dnb.de.

ISBN 978-3-03768-276-0
© 2022 by Braun Publishing AG
www.braun-publishing.ch

2nd edition 2023

EDITOR
Chris van Uffelen
EDITORIAL STAFF AND LAYOUT
Caroline Skrabs, Lena Dagenbach
GRAPHIC CONCEPT
Eva Finkbeiner
REPRODUCTION
Bild1 Druck GmbH, Berlin

FRONT COVER BWM Architekten: Salon Sacher,
Vienna
BACK COVER ABOVE: Ippolito Fleitz Group – Identi-
ty Architects: Caffè Belvedere, Stuttgart
BACK COVER BELOW: Studio VOS: Mirage Bistrot,
Berlin